*Spirituality*
*and*
*Moral Theology*

# Spirituality
# and
# Moral Theology

## Essays from a Pastoral Perspective

Edited by
JAMES KEATING, PH.D.


PAULIST PRESS
New York/Mahwah, N.J.

*Cover design by Kokopelli Design Studio*

*Book design by Theresa M. Sparacio*

Library of Congress Cataloging-in-Publication Data

Spirituality and moral theology : essays from a pastoral perspective / edited by James Keating.
    p.   cm.
    Includes bibliographical references.
    ISBN 0-8091-3936-7 (alk. paper)
    1. Christian ethics—Catholic authors. 2. Spirituality—Catholic Church. 3. Pastoral theology—Catholic Church. 4. Catholic Church—Doctrines. I. Keating, James.

BJ1249 .S645 2000
241'.042—dc21

99-088901

Published by Paulist Press
997 Macarthur Boulevard
Mahwah, New Jersey 07430

www.paulistpress.com

Printed and bound in the
United States of America

# Contents

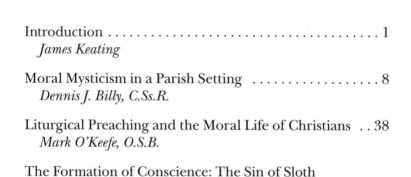

*James Keating, Ph.D.*

# Introduction

Holiness is the goal of all persons who seek to respond to the grace of God offered in the life of Christ. As Christians, we can come to know who we are only in the light of our faith in Christ. The normal route to holiness for the lay Christian is to participate in the paschal mystery through a life embedded within the ordinariness of parish existence. Holiness will be ours only if we go deep into the ordinary without disdain and with faith in God. This is the paradox of holiness: The more we become sanctified, the more we embrace the ordinariness of life as its only context. *Lumen Gentium* declared that in pursuing and attaining holiness, the Christian humanizes the world.[1] Apparently, then, having intimacy with the indwelling God does not remove one from the duties and responsibilities of secular life but is simply its sure foundation. The more Christians appropriate their call to intimacy with God, through the theological and moral virtues, the more they will be able to discern what behaviors and dispositions are "good and pleasing and perfect" (Rm 12:2). In so doing, they become a force for the moral development of the secular world.

1

The purpose of this book is to gather the thoughts of moral theologians on the topic of how being good is related to being holy in the context of pastoral life. It is in dialogue with the principles of spirituality that moral theology will find a renewed voice with which to speak to the current age. We are living in an age of individualism. "Privacy" and "personal choice" reign as absolute norms. This incomplete vision of moral value has brought a predictable reaction from some persons who now call for stricter laws and authoritarian measures of control. Some Catholic moralists, however, are turning to spirituality as a moderating influence, which helps reground the mind and heart not in law and authoritative structures but in devotion, virtue, and the love of God. If we are to promote moral maturity in the church, individualism and authoritarianism need to be replaced with evangelization, re-evangelization, and the pastoral facilitation of moral conversion.

The natural state of reason demands that one thinks and discerns from within a relationship to what one loves. Critiquing the quality, dignity, and completeness of the object of that love is the role of a dynamic spiritual life. This spiritual life, ordered to the love of God and, so ordered, cognizant of the dignity of the human person, can function to purify the mind of loves that are less noble or simply wrong. Our primary formative influences upon character stem from that to which the mind has lovingly attended. We can identify the object of that love, listen to the effects of that love upon our character and choices, and then, if necessary, alter what we love to be more in line with the dignity of a life lived according to the mind of Christ. St. Paul has said it well: "Finally...whatever is honorable, whatever is just, whatever is pure, whatever is lovely, whatever is gracious, if there is any excellence and if there is anything worthy of praise, think about these things" (Phil 4:8f).

Elsewhere he states, "I have been crucified with Christ; yet I live, no longer I, but Christ lives in me" (Gal 2:19–20).

The Christian spiritual life is one lived by means of an awareness of our death in Christ and by our hope for resurrection. This loving attention to God in Christ marks our character deeply. Christian moral discernment is exercised through a character that is disposed to be affected by God. The Christian moral life is not a life of teeth-gritting drudgery. It has its struggles as we grow from viciousness to virtue, but, with the assistance of the indwelling Spirit, it can indeed be a light burden. As Aquinas taught: "The law is said to restrain the hand not the mind since someone who abstains from sin through fear of a penalty does not, simply speaking, withhold his consent to sin, as does someone who abstains from sin for love of justice. And for this reason the new law, which is the law of love, is said to restrain the mind."[2] This understanding of the moral life highlights that Christian ethics is first and foremost a transformation of the believer by grace.

The Catholic adult moral life in the context of Christian spirituality moves the focus from external constructs to internal appropriations of what is true and good, for it is from within a person that evil comes forth...."From the heart come evil thoughts, murder, adultery, unchastity, theft, false witness, blasphemy" (cf. Mt 15:11, 19). The interiorization of moral living has nothing to do with privatism or a masked narcissism; the fruit of an authentic moral-spiritual life always has public effects. It is a life that carries an invitation to the believer to give witness in external behavior to the dispositions and virtues held in his or her heart.

The authors of the essays in this book seek to apply their knowledge of the Catholic moral tradition to a broader spiritual and pastoral context, thus assisting both theologians and pastors in reconfiguring the moral project for the next generation of ministers and faithful. The moral tradition is so broad and deep that each generation must reappropriate and retrieve for more sustained reflection those aspects muted by the last generation of ethicists. How Christian spirituality shapes conscience formation, character development, and moral deliberation should now be brought out from the shadow of other projects (e.g., moral methodology, ecclesial authority) that have dominated moral theology since Vatican II. The relation between moral theology and spirituality is not sufficient to sustain the entire content of moral theology, but it is a necessary domain of inquiry that has lain fallow for too long. This collection of essays, it is hoped, will contribute to a new springtime of dialogue just beginning between spirituality and ethics.

We begin this book with an essay by Dennis Billy, C.Ss.R., who sets the tone of the collection by placing the themes of Christian ethics and spirituality in the context of the parish. The formation of people in the fullness of the Christian tradition, including the mystical, will be the impetus to a pastoral ministry that seeks to influence parishioners to embrace their faith experientially and not simply institutionally. Since the parish is where we live our lives in the sometimes "foreign land "of American popular culture, Billy argues that we need to deepen the parishioner's awareness of his or her Christian vocation. In this deepening awareness resides the roots of the moral mystical life. By tracing some historical influences that led to the separation of the moral and mystical life, Billy recovers their relatedness in the context of the real lives of people who live out of the word, the Eucharist, trinitarian theology, and the experience of small group commitments. The parish will no longer be viewed as a place "to go," but as a gathering of believers to be formed in faith and sent on mission. This mission is both spiritual and moral; in fact, evangelization is that acceptance of the good news that converts the heart to

Christ's heart so that one's moral behavior flows out of such heart-to-heart dialogue.

Mark O'Keefe, O.S.B., specifies further the role of the parish in his essay on liturgical preaching. Primarily, the preacher is to connect the fundamentals of faith to the circumstances of ordinary life. In this way the preacher sheds light upon and assists in revealing the grace of daily commitments. The preacher is to invite the people to regular conversion toward holiness. This call is to come forth from the word of God as interpreted by the homilist. Ideally the people come to recognize their own struggle with vice and so embrace the moral teachings of the church in faith as a way to the holiness they desire. In this way, the skilled preacher introduces the moral life as relevant and attainable through grace in the ordinariness of life. Both spirituality and morality present themselves to parishioners as one life to be lived by all the faithful. As O'Keefe notes, "the proclamation of the Word of God and its interpretation in the act of preaching announces again the Good News of the divine self-offering in Jesus Christ. It demands a response in prayer and in living...and a response that is lived out every day in the ordinary encounters, decisions, and relationships that make up the daily lives of Christian men and women" (p. 50).

For Kenneth Himes, O.F.M., the key moral work to be accomplished in the parish is the formation of conscience. Much time has been spent on that aspect of conscience that involves decision making. What has been muted is the more fundamental aspect of the formation of conscience as Christian. Through the theme of sloth, Himes analyzes why the formation of conscience has been sidelined and "hardness of heart" has taken the ascendancy in some believers. He wonders why we have become apathetic toward the good and how we can come to care again about being good and choosing rightly. Here Himes connects morality and spirituality at their core: "It is by having God move within us that we experience a rebirth of desire and care" (p. 66). The spiritual life assists the moral life by interiorizing its roots in prayer and by pointing to the relative value of moral achievements before the absolute love and mercy of God. This relativizing of moral achievement opens the way for the parishioner to entrust himself or herself totally to God. "Disciples are not in love with 'truth' or the 'good'—they are in love with a personal God who is truth and goodness" (p. 69). We cannot assume one has formed conscience well, but instead invite believers into the depth of meaning that is their identity in Christ. This formation will yield a moral life with profoundly spiritual roots, roots strong enough to feed the passion one needs to do the good in love.

Edward Vacek, S.J., explores the meaning of gratitude to God. He critiques those theologians who would place gratitude at the core of moral living and instead argues that it is love which holds the central place in Christian virtue. Gratitude certainly has a place in one's relationship to God, but this must be held in tension with compassion for the poor, who seemingly have little or nothing for which to be grateful to God. He notes that our principal response to God's love is not to be  thanksgiving, but to love God in return and to love those whom God loves. Since we know that God has a special love for the poor, the Christian can assist them as a sign of the presence of God among us. Ultimately, God wants not our thanks but our hearts, our very selves, given over to God in worship and service.

In her essay, Pamela Smith, SS.C.M., integrates the themes of the previous essays into a meditation upon what criteria exist for living a life of moral goodness and holiness. Through narratives about real Catholics and how the themes of hunger, imagination, gratitude, passion, prodigality, and solidarity emerge from those lives, and from the reflections of the previous authors, Smith summarizes and integrates the themes of this book into a call for the parish to become a center of holiness and formation in Christian conscience.

Taken together, these chapters further the developing conversation in Catholic moral theology on its relationship to spirituality. They further this conversation by specifying the context of this integration in the place where true moral and spiritual formation must occur if Catholics are to embrace the universal call to holiness intrinsic to their baptisms: the parish.

I would like to thank Elizabeth Kampmeier, M.Div., Research Assistant in the School of Theology at the Pontifical College Josephinum, for her generous assistance in the preparation of this book.

## NOTES

1. Catholic Church, Vatican Council II, *Lumen Gentium* (Dogmatic Constitution on the Church), 31. See, for example, Austin Flannery, ed., *Vatican Council II: The Conciliar and Post Conciliar Documents* (Wilmington, Del.: Scholarly Resources, 1975).

2. Thomas Aquinas, *Summa Theologiae (ST)* Ia-IIae q.107 a.1 ad 2. See, for example, *Summa Theologica,* 3 vol. ([New York:] Benziger Brothers, 1947–48).

*Dennis J. Billy, C.Ss.R.*

# Moral Mysticism in a Parish Setting

66 T he devout Christian of the future will either be a 'mystic,' one who has 'experienced' something, or he will cease to be anything at all."[1] When he wrote these words, Karl Rahner was hoping that, in time, the experiential dimensions of Christian faith would somehow allay the deep sense of restlessness that had arisen among believers just after the close of the Second Vatican Council. In doing so, he was trying to remind his readers of the call each of them had to a deep, intimate relationship with God. At the same time, he was also trying to highlight the essential moral character of this relationship, since a mysticism inimical or indifferent to love is not worthy of the name "Christian." The stark possibilities presented by Rahner's jarring, "either/or" statement may very well have been intended to stir emotion and, in hindsight, may well prove to be prophetic. Now, more than thirty years later and at the dawn of a new millennium, one wonders not so much if his words have actually come to pass (something that would be difficult, if not impossible, to determine), but just what they might mean today for the

8

majority of American Catholics whose primary experience of church still unfolds in the context of their local parish.

In this essay, I will propose that a certain type of mysticism (what philosophers describe with the qualifying adjective "moral") has very much to do with the routine, often mundane circumstances of daily parish life. I will argue that "moral mysticism in a parish setting" has deep roots in the Christian tradition and, when adequately retrieved, may well point out a way our future efforts in catechesis and evangelization should take. My aim is to provide an alternative understanding of the way moral and spiritual development is normally conceived and carried out in the local parish setting. This alternative transcends the traditional distinctions among the theological disciplines and focuses on an experiential approach to God at each stage of a person's sojourn through life.

## THE MEANING OF MORAL MYSTICISM

Mysticism can be moral or amoral, concerned or unconcerned with the ethical value of human action. When it is *moral*, it leads to involvement in social issues and/or to specific ethical tasks to which the individual experiences a call; when *amoral*, it means that the individual is unconscious of or simply disregards his or her moral obligations.[2] When viewed under this rather precarious ethical spotlight, mysticism has a stark "either/or" quality about it. I bring this out early in my discussion simply to point out that a bond between mystical experience and ethical behavior does not exist out of necessity: Sometimes the two are related, sometimes not. The basis of that relationship stems from the nature of the mystical experience itself and whether it encourages the person to engage the world constructively through the physical, emotional, intellectual, spiritual, and social dimensions of human existence. The wide range of attitudes toward moral behavior present in some of the current New Age philosophies easily demonstrates this claim, as does the ambivalent attitude toward moral behavior found in many of those seeking pure states of altered consciousness. Christian mysticism, on the other hand, is an entirely different matter, since it leads an individual to actively pursue personal and/or social commitments of a loving (and therefore moral) nature. According to William Johnston, S.J., "mysticism that is not rooted in and grounded in love cannot be called Christian."[3] William McNamara, O.C.D., is even more emphatic. For him, "A Christianity that is not basically mystical must become either a political ideology or a mindless fundamentalism."[4] He goes on to describe two distinct elements of this mystical experience: "(1) the vision of God loved and (2) the moral transformation of the lover who with a wild and relentless passion desires to become identified and equated with the Beloved."[5]

All this is well and good. But what precisely do we mean by "mysticism?" Is it reserved only for those who have risen to the heights of spiritual ecstasy? Can the ordinary Christian ever hope to enjoy a deep awareness of the presence of God in his or her life? Ewert Cousins distinguishes between *spirituality,* a broader term focusing on that deepest part of a person that is open to a transcendent dimension, and *mysticism,* a narrower term pointing to specific moments in a person's life when the transcendent is experienced "with an ecstatic or rapturous intensity."[6] While the distinction is useful for academic purposes and while Cousins readily agrees that the terms overlap and reflect points along a wide range of human experience, I wonder if it does not also tend to perpetuate an elitist view of mystical experience, placing it somehow beyond the reach of ordinary Christians and, in doing so, relegating their own genuine spiritual experiences to a lower status. Language, after all, helps to shape human consciousness. A hesitancy to characterize a person's genuine spiritual experience as "mystical" or at least as tending toward the mystical may unwittingly lead him or her to sense that this particular opening of human experience is closed off and sealed tight. For this reason, I prefer Johnston's definition of authentic Christian mysticism as "a living of the Gospel at a deep level of consciousness."[7] For him, "the Christian mystic is one who lives the Christ-mystery and is transformed by it."[8] This transformation takes place through one's immersion in what Johnston terms the three sources of the Christian mystical experience: "(1) the Word of God in sacred scripture, (2) the sacraments, particularly the Eucharist, and (3) the Word of God in the community called church."[9] This approach roots Christian mysticism in the life of the Christian community and has much to offer our present discussion. It presents mystical experience as good news, as something accessible to all. It describes mysticism not in terms of ecstasy but as a deepening awareness of one's Christian vocation, something to which all of God's people are called.

Other Catholic authors sound the same note. "Mysticism," for Rahner, "is not confined to the privileged few," but is "the truly dynamic element in the Church."[10] For Thomas Merton, "[t]o be a Christian is to be committed to a largely mystical life."[11] For him, mysticism is "the only cure for the angst of modern man."[12] For George Maloney, S.J., "[t]rue contemplation should never be considered as something given only to exceptionally talented psychic mystics."[13] For McNamara, mysticism is "an experience every one of us should know first hand."[14] When seen in this light, we all have a mystical vocation that promises to lead us one day to an intimate, face-to-face encounter with God. Whether we experience this in this life or the next makes very little difference. What is important is that we continually strive to come to a deeper and deeper awareness of God's presence in our lives. We are called to be mystics. This is good news!

We should let others know about this. We should proclaim it! And we should do so especially in the parish setting.

## SOJOURNERS IN A FOREIGN LAND

Moral mysticism, as I have just described it, goes to the very heart of what parish life is about. Everyone in the local parish setting has a deep inner yearning for God. It is part of human nature; we were made that way. If that were not the case, most of us involved in active ministry would be out of work. It is our job to respond to these deep human longings. The parish is one of the primary places where those yearnings are recognized and dealt with constructively. The problem is that sometimes we are so close to certain experiences that we find it difficult to see their true significance. I think that is the way it is with our experience of "parish." This word and the reality it signifies accompany one throughout his or her Catholic life. From cradle to grave, the ordinary occurrences in life as well as the major turning points take place with some reference to the local parish. "What parish do you belong to? "I went to a parochial school." "How was the parish social the other night?" How easily the word and its various cognates come to our lips—almost without thinking. But what does the word mean? Why do we use the word *parish* and not *assembly* or *community* or *body,* or any one of a number of valid and perhaps even more attractive terms that come from our rich tradition? What images come to mind when you say the word?

The word *parish* has deep scriptural roots. It comes from the Greek word *paroikia,* which in the Septuagint meant living in a foreign land without civil or domestic rights. Later, the Jews used it to refer to their exile in Egypt and, still later, to their entire life in this world, which they thought of as a stay in a foreign country. Early Christians used this same concept to refer to the earthly life of the Christian community whose true country and citizenship was in heaven (cf. 1 Pt 1:17).[15] This root meaning of *parish* as "sojourners in a foreign land" must be retrieved from our tradition and embedded in our minds so that it becomes the word's primary meaning for us. Even though the term underwent development over time, taking on a primarily juridic meaning in the context of church administration, this root meaning still holds true today. If it has been forgotten by most Catholics, it needs to be remembered and proclaimed once again with great conviction.

What is more, this fundamental meaning of *parish* goes together nicely with the notion of moral mysticism I have developed above. As Catholics, we relate to one another and to the world through a local parish setting. We live out our lives in and through the context of community. We seek to serve the world and love it through our personal and communal witness. We seek to build up the kingdom here in our midst and strive so that peace and justice will one day reign in our little corner of the earth—and beyond. We also have a sense, however, that this is not our real home, that we are being called elsewhere. We are *in* the world, but not *of* it. We are citizens of heaven and, at times, even get a glimpse of what that life will be like. We all seek to live the gospel on deeper and deeper levels of consciousness. Our use of the word *parish* reminds us of the teleological dimensions of the Christian faith and our communal call to beatitude. All of us yearn for home; we all long to see God face to face. We are moral mystics by baptism, by faith, by vocation. That is what Rahner was getting at. And he is in good company. No lesser theologians than Augustine and Aquinas in the West, and Athanasius and Gregory of Nyssa in the East, hold largely the same view.[16]

## SETTLING FOR LESS

If I seem to be painting too bright a picture for the depth of spiritual experience that can be experienced in the local parish setting, perhaps it is because we have all along been setting our expectations far too low. Perhaps we have become so used to thinking about parish life in a certain way that we find it hard to imagine other enticing (and just as challenging) possibilities for it. Perhaps we have focused so much on the basic requirements of the Christian faith (what C. S. Lewis called "*mere* Christianity"[17]) that we have forgotten about the great heights to which we have all been called. Perhaps we have settled for less for so long that we would not know how even to begin setting our sights on higher goals. I cannot help but think that part of the difficulty faced in parish ministry today comes from our willingness to settle consistently for the least common denominator of the Christian message rather than probing the spiritual depths of the richness our Catholic tradition offers us. Perhaps the great Dominican scholar, Reginald Garrigou-LaGrange, was right: "If we demand too little of ourselves, this is because we do not count sufficiently on grace, because we do not sufficiently ask for it."[18] Perhaps we have somehow forgotten "that God is in us and with us."[19]

How did we get this way? To my mind, it is due to the convergence of two strong theological currents that had a great impact on the direction and shape that parish ministry had taken in the centuries prior to Vatican II, and to which, even today, we are still clinging. I am referring to the "lower class" status assigned to the laity throughout much of the church's history, and to the separation of moral and spiritual theology that began in the late medieval period (perhaps as early as the mid-fourteenth century) and which only recently is being redressed in theological circles. While each of these currents has already been well researched and documented,[20] their interaction over time and the effect they had on parish life and ministry have not. I will leave to others the laborious task of mapping out these admittedly complex historical relationships. For the moment, all I can do is propose a simple working hypothesis: The convergence of these two currents in the local parish setting moved mysticism from the center to the periphery of Catholic lay experience and forced the laity to live out their religious convictions almost exclusively as a response to the moral and legal obligations placed upon them by some higher spiritual authority. If this hypothesis is correct, then it raises some serious questions for pastoral ministers today, who, even after the ground-shaking theological changes wrought by Vatican II, still insist on settling for less even while the people themselves are asking and looking for more.

To unpack my hypothesis, it is important to recall that "discipleship" is the fundamental Christian vocation and that the notion of "states of life" (i.e., priestly, lay, religious) was something that emerged gradually in the church's consciousness.[21] The theology of Vatican II used the theme of "the universal call to holiness" as a way of integrating this primordial call (i.e., "discipleship") with the more specific understandings of vocation (i.e., the various "states of life").[22] In doing so, it sought to recast its previous understanding of vocation, which was based more on the principle of inclusion/exclusion than on the notion of response. This development has a long history. Beginning in late antiquity and continuing down through the centuries of the church's history until the dawn of Vatican II, the superior status afforded the religious life had the converse effect of minimizing the lay state as an authentic way to holiness. While not officially excluded from the quest for holiness, the laity were made all too well aware of their second class status within the church. They were reminded frequently of how the attractions of the world could lure them off the narrow way that leads to salvation. To find God, one needed to cast off the burdens of possessions, marriage, and self will and profess the religious vows of poverty, chastity, and obedience. It was simply taken for granted that the lay state was not conducive to the pursuit of holiness and that the large majority of lay people would lose their souls. These attitudes became deeply ingrained in the spiritual mindset of the faithful and have proven very difficult to root out.

The inferior status of the laity was further emphasized by the physical separation of these two states of life: religious in monasteries and convents, the laity in parishes. This physical distance rested on the assumption that the sacred needed to be separated from what could possibly contaminate it, and it implied a corresponding distance in spiritual discipline. Monks and other religious sought to climb the ladder of spiritual experience through a life of asceticism and contemplative prayer; the laity, in turn, fulfilled their obligations as best they could and begged for God's mercy through pious devotions. Although exceptions certainly existed (e.g., Catherine of Siena, Joan of Arc), the laity by and large did not think of themselves as having access to mystical experience. The profound depths of spiritual experience were considered the domain of the religious life and perhaps also the clergy, who, since the time of the Gregorian reform in the eleventh century, had been largely modeled along religious lines.[23]

All of this was exacerbated by the breakdown of the medieval synthesis achieved by Thomas Aquinas and the subsequent division of theology into various disciplines and subdisciplines.[24] The division between moral theology and spiritual theology has special significance for our topic. Ascetical and mystical theology, the two subdisciplines of spiritual theology, mapped out the way of perfection that religious were to occupy themselves with; moral theology, by way of contrast, focused on one's obligations before God and the church and was as far up the hierarchical ladder of sanctity that the laity could ever hope to ascend. Spiritual theology presupposed moral theology and was lived out in the context of the monastery and convent; moral theology found its home in the confessional and provided the theological rationale for the pastoral care given the laity in the local parish setting. Because of this hierarchical distribution of spiritual states, mystical experience among the laity was thought of as highly unlikely and, whenever instances did occur, was rarely (if ever) taken seriously. Cut off from the rich spiritual treasures of the church, it is not surprising that the laity would seek alternative ways of interpreting and dealing with their spiritual experiences. At their worst, such expressions were condemned by church officials as outright heresy; at their best, they were labeled as innocuous superstitions or esoteric doctrines to be scrutinized with care.[25]

## THE PARISH SETTING AND THE NEW AGE

With the documents of the Second Vatican Council, the Catholic Church has surpassed the "two-tiered" mentality that had cast the religious life as a superior state of life to that of the lay state. Even references in recent magisterial documents to "objective superiority" are nuanced in such a way so that the universal call to holiness is carefully preserved.[26] In post-Vatican II theology, each state of life—lay, religious, priestly—has its own area of competence (and hence can from a certain perspective be considered superior to the others) and is a genuine way to holiness. What is more, each can be thought of as complementing the others, just as the members of the body work together to further the goals of the entire organism (cf. 1 Cor 12:12–30). Recent years have also seen attempts at overcoming the strict divisions between spiritual and moral theology.[27] The developing academic discipline of spirituality promises to be a locus where the tensions with regard to both method and content in the older theological nomenclature can be resolved, the result being the transformation of the strict hierarchical relationship between the disciplines that had characterized so much of pre-Vatican II theology to a more circular (or spiraling) one between spiritual experience and moral responsibility.[28] As it faces the new millennium, Catholic theology is poised for an important reintegration of its spiritual and moral traditions. To my mind, the term *moral mysticism* is one way in which this process of retrieval and integration can be framed, understood, and implemented in a local parish setting.

Something is needed, after all, to jump-start the response of the local parish to the deep longings that are surfacing in the general population. The various expressions of the New Age movement may be seen as shallow and perhaps even faddish attempts to deal with these longings—but at least they are trying. The noticeable drift in the general population away from institutional religion shows that major churches are not satisfying the spiritual hungers of the people. As sociologist Robert Bellah and his coworkers pointed out over a decade ago: "To be effective...the church tradition in the United States would have to be revitalized by taking seriously the criticisms of it by sectarian and mystical religion."[29] More recently, Frank X. Tuoti has put a very direct question to the present crisis in American Catholic life: "Why is it that we are not instructed in the ways of meditation *as central to personal and parish life,* without which a profound, contemplative spirituality cannot be accessed?"[30] His response touches the core of our dilemma, but may be a little hard for some of us to swallow: "If there are few contemplatives in our parishes," he says, "it is because most are content to remain 'conventional Christians,'" who "secretly assure themselves that if they attend to the prescribed externals, go regularly to church, and don't go off the deep end, they are pleasing to God (although in fact they are pleasing mostly to themselves)."[31] No wonder so many younger Catholics have dabbled in the occult and esoteric philosophies of the New Age. What else can we expect? They have done so largely because they are not aware of the rich spiritual tradition available to them in their own Catholic heritage. They are tired of what "conventional Christianity" has to offer. They have been fed the bare minimum for so long and have simply decided to find nourishment for their souls elsewhere.

Today's typical American parish needs to place the riches of the church's spiritual traditions at the center, not on the periphery, of its life. The Eucharist, the visible mandala that points to the even more mysterious mandala of the Trinity, should be the focal point of any such attempt.[32] For this to happen, it needs to be presented in such a way that each anthropological dimension of human existence—the physical, the emotional, the intellectual, the spiritual, and the social—is sensitively addressed and cared for. I realize that this is not an easy thing to accomplish, especially because psychologists remind us that there are different types of personalities, as well as various stages in moral and faith development.[33] The great richness of the Catholic tradition, however, has a little something for everyone and, when thoughtfully studied and presented, promises to meet people where they are, enables them to experience God in a manner that fits their personality, addresses their level of spiritual and moral maturity, and readies them to come back for more.

## RE-IMAGINING THE PARISH

Another way of looking at the situation would be to speak of the "paradigmatic shift" that has taken place over the past thirty years in the Church's understanding of the vocational states of life and the theological disciplines, but which has up until now had very little practical impact on the self-understanding of its most basic institutions. To be even more precise, the theological and pastoral justification for speaking of moral mysticism in a parish setting has existed in the Church's teaching for quite some time, but has yet even to get on (let alone past) the diocesan or parish council drawing board. This should not surprise us since, as Avery Dulles aptly points out, institutions provide continuity and stability in the midst of change but often at the cost of critical and creative thinking.[34] Resistance to change is often a good (we call it "courage"), but under certain conditions it can also cause an institution to harden and atrophy. If care is not taken, it can work against the institution's ability to adapt to changing times and to maintain its credibility for those it seeks to serve. When this happens, such institutions reach a critical point in their history and face one of three possibilities: extinction, minimal survival, or revitalization.

I believe that many parishes in the United States have reached this critical juncture and will have to face some hard choices in the future. Many will dwindle away in numbers until extinction becomes the most reasonable alternative. Many more will be content with minimal survival and continue to have little or no impact on the lives of those who live within their boundaries. A very small number will seek to revitalize their communities in keeping with the paradigm shift I have just briefly outlined.[35] To do so, these parishes will need to re-imagine themselves in the light of their origins as a sojourning people destined one day to behold the face of God. I would like to suggest that this process of "re-imagining" needs to take place on three levels: the symbolic, the relational, and the practical.

### 1. The Symbolic

Every parish community projects an array of images both inwardly to members and outwardly to the world. This is done both consciously and unconsciously and constitutes what we can call its guiding "vision" or "self-image." Most parishes, I would venture to say, suffer from a poor self-image: They expect little of themselves because they feel they have so little to give.[36] Parishes will not be able to foster change among their members if they do not reverse such feelings of inferiority and present the vision of moral mysticism as an intimate part of their own self-understanding. This means going back to the root meaning of parish as "sojourners in a foreign land" and making sure that parishioners both understand and accept it as a part of their parish identity. In my mind, seven images in particular will help to communicate this meaning: displacement, journey, companionship, food, story, commemoration, and rest. Journey is the root metaphor and provides the underlying context for the other six. I am aware that "the idea of journey," in the words of Arthur W. Frank, "has become a New Age spice sprinkled indiscriminately to season almost any experience."[37] But I am also aware of how deeply rooted it is in the Judeo-Christian tradition and how, when combined with the sphere of the sacred, it takes on the dimensions of pilgrimage. Members of the local parish community need to be reminded that they are like "strangers in a foreign land,"[38] who have embarked on a perilous journey that will lead them from their experience of displacement through the heights and depths of human experience to the threshold of the sacred. They need to look upon one another as companions on this journey, who break bread together, share their stories, commemorate life's joys and sorrows, and rest in the security of God's love for them. They need to have a sense of their common destination and share the conviction of one day arriving there and resting in God. What is more, they need to have a sense that Jesus is Emmanuel (i.e., "God with us," cf. Is 7:14; Mt 1:23), their silent companion every step of the way.

What needs to be communicated to the parishioners is that this journey is unlike any they have ever experienced before. They are going home, but barely remember what home is like. Like strangers in a foreign land, they have a strong sense of living in two cities (to borrow some imagery from Augustine[39]), belonging yet not belonging to the world they live in. This very sense of displacement, moreover, gives them a different outlook toward life and toward death. As "sojourners in a foreign land," they journey toward God as they proclaim God's presence in their midst; they announce the coming of the kingdom and find in their lives of service a concrete expression of its arrival; they experience God's presence in their midst as well as God's absence. Like the disciples on the road to Emmaus, their hearts burn within them as Jesus walks beside them on the road, explains the scriptures to them, and reveals himself in the breaking of the bread (Lk 24:13–35). None of this should be new to their ears, but it all needs to be emphasized with renewed vigor. For moral mysticism in a parish setting to succeed, these images must be among the first to come to mind whenever the parishioners think of their local church.

## 2. The Relational

Throughout this journey through a foreign land, parish communities mediate the world to their members by helping them to interpret it, make informed judgments about it, and interact with it. This process of mediation is ultimately concerned with forming right relationships and is intimately connected with each person's spiritual journey. There are many levels to the world we live in, and it is important that parishes strive to take all of them into account. There are obviously many ways of doing so, each with their obvious strengths and weaknesses. I am particularly struck by what Fredrica R. Halligan calls the six levels of *conjunctio,* where union with God takes place in: (1) the personal, (2) the bipersonal, (3) the small group, (4) humanity itself, (5) our image(s) of God, and (6) mystery.[40] The first has to do with the quest for inner wholeness and the deep experience of the divine toward which it tends; the second, with the spiritual union between two people; the third, with the deep sense of unity and solidarity that can be experienced among small gatherings of people; the fourth, with the sense of oneness with all of humanity (and, I would add, with the world); the fifth, with the convergence and ultimate transcendence of our various images of God; and the sixth, with the encounter with mystery itself. These levels are not "stages" in mystical experience as such, but a spiraling movement of ever deeper experiences of consciousness and union with the Divine. Although they are used by Halligan to explain mystical experience within the general framework of Jungian psychology, they do not seem to be tied of necessity to this or any particular school of psychology or spirituality—not even to the upward spiraling movement, for that matter. For our present purposes, they provide us with a helpful way of explaining the various levels of the world we live in and what moral mysticism might mean for us in the local parish setting. They do this first and foremost by shifting the focus of mystical experience from the exclusively personal emphasis associated with it so often in the past to a variety of levels of consciousness that each of us in some way shares in by virtue of our being members of the mystical body of Christ. When coupled with what we already know about personality types and the continuum of moral and faith development, we can conclude that Christian mysticism (i.e., "living the gospel on a deep level of consciousness") lends itself to a variety of expressions and is "moral" precisely because it seeks right relationship on each of these levels.

## 3. The Practical

Having a vision of parish as a community of "sojourners in a foreign land" and a knowledge of the various levels of the world in which we live will not, of itself, insure an atmosphere of moral mysticism. Concrete steps need also be taken. What follows is a series of practical suggestions that can assist people in achieving these aims in a local parish setting. For clarity's sake, I follow the six levels of *conjunctio* discussed above.

*Personal:* To begin with, each parish member should be encouraged to reflect upon his or her personal journey with God. For this to happen, opportunities need to be created where individuals can gather to talk about their experiences in a free, nonthreatening atmosphere. Giving a person the opportunity to give a "witness story" of how he or she has experienced God can do much to edify both the individual and the community. Priests should be encouraged to share their personal experiences of God from the pulpit; religious educators should be encouraged to do so in class; the traditional means of parish communication (e.g., parish bulletins, newsletters, web sites) could provide space for such sharing.

In addition to personal testimony, opportunities could be provided for spiritual direction so that interested individuals could examine their life of prayer in the presence of trained individuals. Lists should be available of competent spiritual directors in the area. Perhaps a program of group spiritual direction could be initiated in the parish. Spiritual reading should be encouraged, especially the great mystics of the church (e.g., Julian of Norwich, the author of The Cloud of Unknowing, Teresa of Avila, John of the Cross—to name but a few). Every parish should also have a resource library (or at least a bibliography) listing books that would be particularly helpful in the various stages of life and spiritual development. Classes and practicums could be offered in the various types of prayer, and these could be related to the liturgy, especially the Eucharist and the sacrament of reconciliation. The dynamic relationship between contemplation and conversion could be emphasized, pointing out especially how the former helps root out the tendency we all have toward sin. In all of this, care should be taken to emphasize the integration in a person's life of the five basic dimensions of human existence: the physical, the emotional, the intellectual, the spiritual, and the social.

*Bipersonal:* God can also be experienced in human friendship. As far as I know, very little is being done in the parish setting to help friends to understand how God may be an integral part of their relationship. Small encounter groups of various kinds of committed friends (e.g., singles, engaged couples, married couples, and other kinds of friends) could be set up with opportunities to discuss the strengths, tensions, and difficulties of the relationship. If this seems too threatening, then perhaps a lecture series could be offered that would address different types of friendship and the various stages involved in a deep, intimate relationship founded on Christ. At the very least, the three major characteristics of friendship—benevolence, reciprocity, and mutual indwelling—should be raised and considered. The literature on these relationships should be made available and priests should not steer away from discussing them in their Sunday preaching. Even small gestures can have a great impact on a local parish. A discussion group on Aelred of Riveaulx's *Spiritual Friendship* might help people understand a little more clearly how their relationship with their friends affects their relationship with God—and vice versa. Well chosen excerpts of this work could appear in the parish bulletin. Efforts should be made to raise the awareness of parishioners that the friendships they share have an important role to play in their spiritual lives. At appropriate moments in a parish life (e.g., a silver wedding jubilee, a retirement party), close friends could be given the opportunity to speak of how much their friendships mean to them. All this could be done with great lightness and humor, while still getting the main point across: exploring the various ways in which friends can help each other grow in the spiritual life.

*The Small Group:* Living the gospel on a deep level of consciousness can also be facilitated in small groups. Ideally, the Sunday liturgies will convey a sense of intimacy and solidarity in the local parish. If the numbers are too large for this take place, the staff should seriously consider breaking the parish up into smaller focus groups of twenty to twenty-five people. These small "base" communities could be instrumental in creating in the parish as a whole a sense of welcoming and hospitality that will radiate to members and visitors alike. Jesus himself instructs his disciples to welcome strangers (Mt 25:35), and it should be a priority of any parish that views itself as "strangers in a foreign land." If this format does not seem feasible, then the staff might wish to look at the various groups and societies that already exist in the parish and try to find ways in which this spiritual dimension can be brought to the fore. This might be very easy to do in a prayer group, but perhaps much more difficult with the finance committee, parish council, or weekly Bingo crew. I am not suggesting that the nature of the groups be changed or even that a lot of superfluous things be done, but one would be surprised how a short moment of silence or some short breathing exercises done in unison with the Jesus Prayer can change the whole tenor of a meeting. When God is consciously invited into and made a part of a small group experience, the common humanity of that group comes to the fore and changes the way conclusions are determined and decisions implemented. Simply invoking his name will make a difference. Jesus himself said: "Where two or three are gathered together in my name, there am I in the midst of them" (Mt 18:20).

*Humanity:* Local parishes look not only inward toward their own inner personal, bipersonal, and small group relationships, but also outward to the entire world. The evolving global consciousness has caused many American parishes to become more sensitive to issues of peace and justice in other areas of the world, especially in developing countries. Conscious of this important level of human experience, the United States bishops recently sent out a call to global solidarity to all their parishes. While American Catholics have traditionally been very generous in sharing their resources with the needy, much more needs to be done "to integrate more fully the international dimensions of Catholic discipleship within a truly universal church."[41] The local parish can be instrumental in raising awareness of such needs (both human and environmental) and in offering practical ways in which individuals and entire parishes can help. It can also help people draw the deeper connections of solidarity with humanity, the earth, and God—the three basic concepts involved in all mature theological reflection.[42] Parishes need to inspire their members not only to contribute money but also to work and to pray for solidarity among themselves, with other Christian churches, other religions, and all peoples of the world. The parish can help to personalize these needs by choosing specific projects in which the entire parish community can become involved. There are so many needs that sometimes people become numb to what is happening around them. By filtering these needs, prioritizing them, and making a concerted effort to deal with *some* of them, parishioners can make a real difference in the world. Linking these social or environmental projects to liturgies or ecumenical prayer services would be a good way of emphasizing the spiritual dimension of human and world solidarity. This is moral mysticism at its best! By raising awareness in these areas and by taking concrete steps to build bonds of solidarity, the local parish brings both its people and the world a little closer to God's dream for humanity.

*Our Image(s) of God:* As our experience of God deepens, we eventually come up against the limitations of human language. That is not to say that our images of God and the formulation of faith are void of authentic meaning.

It only means that we begin to see how much greater God is than the words we use to convey our beliefs in and experiences of the Divine. Traditional Catholic theology uses the terms *kataphatic* (or positive) and *apophatic* (or negative) theology to describe what human language can and cannot do in describing one's experience of God. Mystics convey their experiences through words and images, but often find that these fall far short of the *"nada,"* the "nothing," the great "cloud of unknowing" they are experiencing. Even here, parishes have an important role to play in the spiritual life since, as Johnston points out, we all share in a universal call to mysticism: It is "not for an elite but for everyone," and something that is "included in the grace of baptism."[43] If this is true, then why is it that we do not hear much talk of such experiences? People often experience the threshold of the sacred, but are hesitant to share their experiences, either for lack of words, for lack of ease about what they have experienced, or because they are afraid that others would not understand them. By creating a nonthreatening atmosphere where people can listen to others share such experiences and then perhaps even share their own, parishes can help people to feel more comfortable in naming their experiences of God. Doing so will also help them to realize and feel comfortable with the fact that whatever they say will not do justice to the depth of the experience and the meaning it has for their lives. When they learn that the Catholic tradition has a way of dealing with, handling, and in fact even guiding such deep experiences, people will be more apt to listen to the wisdom of the centuries and allow it to shape their lives.

*Mystery:* Finally, moral mysticism brings a person into an encounter with Mystery. As the contemplative experience deepens in a person's life, distractions gradually disappear and a person gently feels more and more absorbed by the divine presence. To get to this point, people often experience a time of darkness or confusion in their lives. Such periods come, however, not so much to test but to deepen a person's life of faith and to make that person rely more heavily on God. The goal of the mystical life is union with God. This experience can be so deep that the mystic almost feels as though he or she has lost his or her identity. In such instances, the church (and in this case, the local parish) provides a strong corrective to these strong pantheistic leanings. Here, the church guides the way for the mystic, providing the parameters within which he or she can rest securely in the Nameless Unknowing Word of God. We may be tempted to think that parishes will have little to do or say with people who have such experiences. It may very well be true that few are called to the very heights of mystical prayer as described, for example, in the *Interior Castle* of Teresa of Avila or the *Spiritual Canticle* of John of the Cross. Parishes need to get into the habit, however, of meeting people where they are—and then offering them a little bit more. Moral mysticism, in particular, needs strong models to inspire people to lead lives of contemplation and to experience the gifts and fruits to which God is calling them. For this reason, parishes can help people in their spiritual lives simply by keeping the memory of such saints and their deep experiences of God alive. The church seeks to do this through the calendar of the saints and the various saints' days throughout the liturgical year. Yet these are just a handful of the thousands upon thousands of mystics—both living and dead—who have lived the gospel on a deep level of consciousness. The world is held together by mystics who bathe in the experience of the Divine: Some are active; others have little direct contact with the world. This probing, contemplative gaze affects the lives of the entire human family—even the lives of the believing community in the local parish setting.

CONCLUSION

I realize that I have been painting an idealized picture of what a parish can do to respond to the deep spiritual longings of the person in the pew. Ideals, however, are meant to inspire (not depress) and my purpose in all of this is to help us to raise our sights and to give us a sense of the wide range of possibilities of what moral mysticism would mean if it were to be implemented in a parish setting. Behind all of this is the firm conviction that if we continue to use the word parish in our Catholic vocabulary, we need to get back in touch with its original meaning. In the primitive Church, the notion of "parish" went hand in hand with that of a journeying people who experienced God deeply in their lives, that is, what I am referring to as "moral mysticism." These Christians had a deep sense of having one foot in what Augustine would call "the earthly city" and the other in "the heavenly city." Despite nearly two thousand years of cultural, philosophical, and theological achievements in the West, I honestly see no reason why it cannot be so today.

Allow me to put it another way: Thomas Aquinas distinguishes between perfect beatitude, which exists only in heaven when the blessed see God face to face, and imperfect beatitude, which can be experienced in this life and is intimately related to the life of faith, hope, and love.[44] The distinction is a very good one, since it makes quite clear what we can and cannot experience in this life. As often happens in the history of ideas, however, its meaning has often been misrepresented. For a number of complex reasons, some of which I have alluded to earlier, we have for years (perhaps even centuries) been selling the experience of imperfect beatitude short. We have somehow managed to convince ourselves that if we cannot have *all* of the *visio Dei*, then we can have *none* of it. If the beatific vision is postponed until the next life, then we have simply come to believe that we have to work hard, try to do what is right, and wait for it to come. That is not what Aquinas meant, however.[45] The walk of faith, in his mind, brought tangible, concrete results in this life—right now, in the present! The apostle Paul, one of the great evangelists and mystics of the early church, agrees: "Now we are seeing a dim reflection in a mirror; but then we shall see face to face. The knowledge that I have now is imperfect; but then I shall know as fully as I am known. In short, there are three things that last: faith, hope, and love; and the greatest of these is love (1 Cor 13:12-13)."

Moral mysticism is a way of speaking about the experience of God's love in the state of imperfect beatitude. In a parish setting, it is not only possible but essential. As one well-known spiritual writer puts it: "If the schools, churches, and religious communities throughout the country are not at least half full of *earthy mystics*–people who know God by *experience*–then Christianity has failed."[46] Or again: "If the external management of the Church is so demanding that its shepherds become administrators instead of pastors, more concerned with public relations than mystical relations, then Christianity has failed."[47] If parishes wish not merely to survive but to *revitalize* the lives of their members by reaching out to those around them in the spirit of love and Christian service, then they have to re-imagine themselves, implement the paradigm shift that has taken place in Catholic theology over the past generation and a half, get into the habit of meeting people where they are, and offer them a little bit more. The stakes are high, and much is riding on the decisions we make for the future of parish life in America.

Robert E. Duggan puts it this way:

> Despite the absence of much specific effort aimed at parish, either on the official or unofficial level, the parish remains the ecclesial structure that most immediately affects the spiritual vitality of millions of Catholics. To a large extent, the vast renewal of the

Church envisioned at Vatican II will succeed or fail depending on the extent to which parish renewal becomes a reality.[48]

These words highlight both the centrality of the local parish to the church's life and mission and the great need for more concentrated efforts of renewal. Tuoti puts it a slightly different way: "Until our appointed shepherds lead their flocks into the art of 'prayer of the heart' everything will remain pretty much the way it has been over recent centuries— parishes incapable of leading people to deep personal inner transformation, the source of authentic Church renewal."[49]

These quotations provide a fitting framework for understanding the words of Karl Rahner with which I began this essay. If it is true that "the Christian of the future will either be a mystic or nothing at all," then it makes just plain common sense that future efforts of parish renewal should try to tap into the deep mystical yearnings of people's hearts and direct them toward the experience of God. What I have presented concerning moral mysticism in a parish setting is an attempt to envision what such a renewal might look like.


### NOTES

1.  Karl Rahner, "Christian Living Formerly and Today," *Theological Investigations*, vol. 7, trans. David Bourke (London: Darton, Longman & Todd, 1971), 15. For the German original, see "Frömmigkeit Fruher und Heute," *Shriften zur Theologie*, 2nd ed., vol. 7/1 (Einsiedeln. Zurich, Köln: Benziger, 1971), 22. (The first edition appeared in 1966.)

2.  This is not the place to go into the many subtle distinctions scholars make about the nature and forms of mystical experience, but see, for example, James R. Horne, *The Moral Mystic* (Waterloo, Ontario: Canadian Corporation for Studies in Religion, 1983), 26–59; and Dennis J. Billy, "Mysticism and Moral

Theology," *Studia Moralia* 34 (1996): 389–95. On the distinction between moral and amoral, see Horne, *The Moral Mystic*, 29–30, 46–54, 56–59.

3. William Johnston, *Mystical Theology: The Science of Love* (London: HarperCollins, 1996), 61.

4. William McNamara, *The Human Adventure: Contemplation for Everyman* (Garden City, N.Y.: Image, 1976), 25.

5. McNamara, 132.

6. Ewert Cousins, "States of Consciousness: Charting the Mystic Path," in *The Fires of Desire: Erotic Energies and the Spiritual Quest*, eds. Fredrica R. Halligan and John J. Shea (New York: Crossroad, 1992), 128–29.

7. Johnston, *Mystical Theology*, 9.

8. William Johnston, *The Mystical Way: Silent Music and The Wounded Stag* (London: Fount, 1993), 221.

9. Johnston, *The Mystical Way*, 220.

10. Heribert Fischer, "Mysticism," *Encyclopedia of Theology*, ed. Karl Rahner (New York: Seabury Press, 1975), 1005–6.

11. Cited in Frank X. Tuoti, *Why Not Be a Mystic?* (New York: Crossroad, 1996), 20.

12. Cited in Tuoti, 32.

13. George A. Maloney, *Mysticism and the New Age* (New York: Alba House, 1991), 37.

14. McNamara, *Christian Mysticism: A Psychotheology* (Chicago: Franciscan Herald, 1981), 3.

15. Walter Bauer, "Paroikia," *A Greek-English Lexicon of the New Testament and Other Early Christian Literature*, 2nd ed. (revised and augmented from Bauer's 5th edition, 1958), trans. and eds. F. W. Gingrich, F. W. Danker, W. F. Arndt (Chicago and London: University of Chicago Press, 1957, 1979), 629.

16. For mysticism in the thought of the church fathers, see Andrew Louth, *The Origins of the Christian Mystical Tradition: From Plato to Denys* (Oxford: Clarendon, 1981). The chapters on Nicene Orthodoxy and Augustine are especially insightful. For mysticism in Aquinas, see Jan-Jendrik Walgrave, "Prayer and Mysticism," *Communio* 12 (1985): 276–92.

17. He attributes the origin of the phrase to Baxter; see C. S. Lewis, *Mere Christianity* (New York: Macmillan, 1952; paperback ed., 1960), 6.

18. Reginald Garriou-LeGrange, *Christian Perfection and Contemplation* (New York: Herder and Herder, 1937), 91.

19. Garriou-LeGrange, 91.

20. See, for example, Alexandre Faivre, *The Emergence of the Laity in the Early Church*, trans. David Smith (Mahwah, N.J.: Paulist Press, 1990); John Bugge, *Virginitas: An Essay in the History of a Medieval Idea* (The Hague: Martinus Hijhopp, 1975); François Vandenbroucke, "Le divorce entre théologie et mystique," *Nouvelle revue théologique* 72 (1950): 372–89.

21. On discipleship, see Keith Egan, "The Laity's Call to a Spirituality of Discipleship, *The Jurist* 47 (1987): 73–74; William J. Rademacher, *Lay Ministry: A Theological, Spiritual, and Pastoral Handbook* (Middlegreen, Slough: St Paul, 1991), 21–24; on the emergence of the states of life in the church, see Jacques Fontaine, "The Practice of Christian Life: The Birth of the Laity," trans. Jill Raitt, in *Christian Spirituality*, vol. 1, eds. Bernard McGinn, John Meyendorff, in collaboration with Jean Leclercq (New York: Crossroad, 1985), 453–85. See also Faivre, *The Emergence of the Laity*, esp. 3–14.

22. See Catholic Church, Vatican Council II, *Lumen Gentium* (Dogmatic Constitution on the Church), 39–42. See Austin Flannery, ed., *Vatican Council II: The Conciliar and Post Conciliar Documents* (Wilmington, Del.: Scholarly Resources, 1975).

23. For other notable exceptions of lay mysticism during this period, see Jean Leclercq, François Vanderbroucke, and Louis Bouyer, *A History of Christian Spirituality*, vol. 2 (New York: Seabury Press, 1982), 499–505.

24. On the breakdown of the medieval synthesis, see Gordon Leff, *The Dissolution of the Medieval Outlook: An Essay on the Intellectual and Spiritual Change in the Fourteenth Century* (New York: Harper & Row, 1976), esp. 91–92.

25. See, for example, the characteristics of late-medieval lay piety in Leclercq, Vanderbroucke and Bouyer, *A History of Christian Spirituality*, vol. 2, 489–99.

26. See Dennis J. Billy, "'Objective Superiority' in *Vita consecrata*," *Review for Religious* 55 (1996): 640–45.

27. See, for example, Mark O'Keefe, *Becoming Good, Becoming Holy: On the Relationship of Christian Ethics and Spirituality* (Mahwah, N.J.: Paulist Press, 1995); Dennis J. Billy and Donna Lynn Orsuto, eds., *Spirituality and Morality: Integrating Prayer and Action* (Mahwah, N.J.: Paulist Press, 1996); William C. Spohn, "Spirituality and Ethics: Exploring the Connections," *Theological Studies* 58 (1997): 109–23; Marciano Vidal, *Moral y espiritualidad: de la separación a la convergencia* (Madrid: Editorial El Perpetuo Socorro, 1997). See also the issue dedicated to the topic in *The Way Supplement* 88 (Spring 1997).

28. See Sandra M. Schneiders, "Spirituality in the Academy," *Theological Studies* 50 (1989): 676–97, esp. 684–95. Johnston writes that the purgative, illuminative, and unitive ways are deeply intertwined in our lives *(The Mystical Way*, 192). In a similar way, Fredrica R. Halligan asserts that "[r]esearchers into both psychotherapy and the stages of spiritual development today tend to agree with the spiral image of progress" (Fredrica R. Halligan, "Keeping Faith with the Future: Toward Final Conscious Unity," in *The Fires of Desire*, 184).

29. Robert N. Bellah, Richard Madsen, William M. Sullivan, Ann Swidler, and Steven M. Tipton, *Habits of the Heart: Individualism and Commitment in American Life* (New York: Harper & Row Perennial Library, 1986), 247.

30. Tuoti, 36.

31. Tuoti, 48.

32. For the Eucharist as a mandala, see Johnston, *The Mystical Way*, 302–11. For the relationship between the liturgy and the Christian moral life, see O'Keefe, *Becoming Good, Becoming Holy*, 91–109; Jan Michael Joncas, "The Church at Prayer," in Billy and Orsuto, eds., *Spirituality and Morality*, 80–96; Sergio Bastianel, *Prayer in Christian Moral Life*, trans. Bernard Hoose (Middlegreen Slough: St. Paul, 1986), 69–87.

33. Helpful syntheses appear in Owen Flanagan, *Varieties of Moral Personality: Ethics and Psychlogical Realism* (Cambridge, Mass./London: Harvard University Press, 1991); James W. Fowler, *Stages of Faith: The Psychology of Human Development and the Quest of Meaning* (San Francisco: Harper & Row, 1981); Charles M.

Shelton, *Morality of the Heart: A Psychology for the Christian Moral Life* (New York: Crossroad, 1990).

34.  Avery Dulles, *Models of the Church* (Garden City, N.Y.: Image, 1974), 47, 49.

35.  Today, the terms *extinction, minimal survival,* and *revitalization* are used most frequently in relationship to the renewal (or refounding) of religious life. Their wider application to parishes, though not admissible in all details, presents an imposing metaphor for the current spiritual crisis in American Catholic life.

36.  This may explain why "there have been relatively few efforts that are specifically parish-based or whose aim is explicitly parish renewal" (Robert D. Duggan, "Parish, Parish Renewal," *The New Dictionary of Catholic Spirituality*, ed. Michael Downey [Collegeville, Minn.: Liturgical Press, 1993], 717).

37.  Arthur W. Frank, *The Wounded Storyteller: Body, Illness, and Ethics* (Chicago/London: The University of Chicago Press, 1995), 117.

38.  See *Lumen Gentium*, 8.

39.  Augustine of Hippo, *The City of God*, XIX, 17. See, for example, Augustine of Hippo, *The City of God* (New York: Modern Library; Random House, 1950).

40.  Halligan, "Keeping Faith with the Future," 189–94.

41.  Catholic Church, National Conference of Catholic Bishops, "Called to Global Solidarity: International Challenges for U.S. Parishes," *Origins* 27 (1997): 424.

42.  N. Max Wildier, *The Theologian and His Universe: Theology and Cosmology from the Middle Ages to the Present* (New York: Seabury Press, 1982), 1.

43.  Johnston, *Mystical Theology*, 255.

44.  Thomas Aquinas, *Summa Theologiae* I–II, q.4, a.3, resp. See, for example, *Summa Theologica*, 3 vol. ([New York]: Benziger Brothers, 1947–48).

45.  According to Carlo Leget: "In Aquinas' account of happiness, imperfect and perfect *beatitudo* should not be played off against each other. Both name different aspects of the same process. Both find their place within the framework of God bestowing His life in creatures in different modes and degrees; or

more basically: the framework of God's self-communication in the work of creation. One could say that God created man in order to communicate His beatitude: He created beings endowed with intellect and will so as to be known and loved by them." See Carlo Leget, *Living with God: Thomas Aquinas on the Relation between Life on Earth and 'Life' after Death* (Leuven: Peeters, 1997), 147.

46. McNamara, *The Human Adventure*, 184.
47. McNamara, *The Human Adventure*, 185.
48. Duggan, in Downey, ed., 717.
49. Tuoti, 36.

*Mark O'Keefe, O.S.B.*

# Liturgical Preaching and the Moral Life of Christians

Week after week, Sunday after Sunday, Catholics hear the word of God proclaimed and preached in their parish masses. In fact, for many, this weekly ritual is almost the full extent of their encounter with the scriptures for the entire week. What impact does this liturgical preaching have on their daily lives? Or perhaps we should pose a question more possible for a moral theologian to answer: What impact *ought* liturgical preaching to have on the daily lives of Christians, on the decisions they make, on the kinds of people they are becoming, and, ultimately, on their path to an authentic Christian holiness grounded on real moral goodness? This is the fundamental question that guides this essay.

Understanding the influence of liturgical preaching on the moral life of Christians requires the prior understanding of the nature and purpose of preaching (especially within the context of the liturgy) as well as the nature of the Christian moral life. Obviously, how one understands the nature of each will influence how one consequently understands the influence of the one upon the other.[1] After examining, then, the basic nature of both preaching and the moral life, we will be in a better position to suggest the nature of the influence of liturgical preaching on the Christian moral life. Further, since the preacher in the Catholic tradition is most often a priest, I would also like to draw out some implications for the life and ministry of priests as preachers of the word and moral teachers in the church.

Because my focus is on the foundational relationship of preaching to Christian moral formation, I will not address at any length the important but complex question of preaching on specific moral issues nor the even more particular question of a method for preaching on moral questions.[2] Furthermore, of course, although I am a preacher, I am not a homiletician. It is, I trust, with a certain humility that a moral theologian would enter a general discussion of the nature and purpose of preaching—without presuming to venture further into extended comment on methods of preaching on particular types of topics or issues.

## WHAT IS LITURGICAL PREACHING?

In their 1982 reflection on preaching, *Fulfilled in Your Hearing,* the Bishops' Committee on Priestly Life and Ministry offered the following definition of a liturgical homily:

> a scriptural interpretation of human existence which enables a community to recognize God's active presence, to respond to that presence in faith through liturgical word and gesture, and beyond the liturgical assembly, through a life lived in conformity with the Gospel.[3]

As will become clear, this definition already suggests the basic lines of the relationship between liturgical preaching and the moral life of Christians.

Preaching certainly has a number of functions within the life of the church, such as: proclamation, instruction, explanation and interpretation of the Lectionary readings, and exhortation. Before the Second Vatican Council, much of Catholic preaching seemed to be directed at educating the faithful in basic doctrines of the Catholic faith. *The Code of Canon Law* assumes that preaching continues to have at least this catechetical or pedagogical function.[4] At the same time, the renewal of Catholic biblical studies, revealing anew the beauty and depth of the scriptures, and dialogue with the Protestant tradition's emphasis on preaching, has opened up the possibility of a greater richness in preaching for the life of Catholics and of the church.

While preaching has a certain pedagogical function and while particular homilies in particular circumstances may call for a greater degree of instruction, preaching cannot be equated with teaching or catechetics. As the bishops wrote in *Fulfilled in Your Hearing:* "The liturgical gathering is not primarily an educational assembly."[5] Preaching is not primarily a matter of exhortation, either, though it does seek to promote a change in the daily lives of Christians. The exhortative task of preaching, however, follows upon a more basic hermeneutical task as a proclamation of God's word to the actual circumstances of a particular community.

To speak of a fundamentally hermeneutic purpose of preaching presupposes that the preacher must first engage the text to be preached. The tools of modern critical exegesis aid the preacher's interpretation of the biblical text; but preaching must be more than a reporting or summary of the materials in good exegetical commentaries on the scriptures. Simply to report on exegetical commentaries or merely to explain what a biblical text would have meant to its original hearers would leave the full power of the scriptural text and preaching largely untapped. In fact, it would suggest that the full meaning of a biblical text is revealed by discovering, as much as one can, what the text *meant* for a bygone era.

In the end, the preacher seeks to interpret and to proclaim the scriptures so that the biblical word can interpret the lives of the people of God. It is in this way that we can speak of the most basic hermeneutical task of preaching.[6] The preacher interprets and proclaims the word of God, using the tools of modern critical exegesis precisely in the act of allowing it to interpret the lives of the hearers. Said in another way, the preacher seeks to "break open the scriptures" so that the scriptures can "break open" the meaning of our actual life situations. Standing between the biblical word and the actual lives of the hearers, the preacher can be said to be a "mediator of meaning," revealing not so much the meaning of a written text but the meaning of the lives of the hearers in light of that revelatory text.[7]

Authentic and effective preaching, then, requires not only understanding the text but also understanding the world of the hearers, their life situations, their joys and their concerns. The preacher must attend both to the scriptures and to the people, listening for the voice of the Spirit speaking anew in the encounter between the living word of God and the people of God. Homiletic preparation involves, therefore, the immediate tasks of study, prayer, and reflection on the biblical text but also the long-term and consistent task of listening both in prayer and in a real attention to the life and spirit of the community.[8]

Mary Catherine Hilkert, following on the work of Karl Rahner and Edward Schillebeeckx, speaks of preaching as "naming grace" already present in human experience and history.[9] Grace is already and always at work in the context of human life and history. Though most often unrecognized by one's conscious reflection, God is always present in trial and in success, in the joyful and in the tragic, in rejoicing and in grief. Preaching, then, "names" the grace that is present both in the ordinarily mundane lives of the congregation but also in the less common joys and tragedies that they experience from time to time. The act of "naming" is an interpretive task that seeks to understand, in a more basic and more authentic way, the experience and events of the hearers and of the world around them in light of the word of God. Robert Waznak summarizes this point emphatically: "A homily might be exegetically and theologically sound and precise but if it fails to reveal and name grace in the specific context of the listeners' lives, then the Good News is not heard."[10] Preaching, then, can be said to have a profoundly sacramental character in that it seeks to reveal grace present in the ordinary events of human life.[11]

Preaching, of course, can occur in a number of contexts; but preeminent is preaching within the context of the church's liturgy, especially in the eucharistic liturgy.[12] Certainly, it is in the context of the Sunday Eucharist that most Catholics encounter regular preaching. In fact, the Second Vatican Council taught that the homily is an integral part of the liturgy, and it is not to be omitted on Sundays and holy days except for serious reason.[13] This is consistent with the council's teaching that the Liturgy of the Word and the eucharistic action are "so closely connected with each other that they form one single act of worship."[14] In word and in ritual, the Christian community is confronted again with God's gracious self-offer that shines the divine light on the history of their refusal to listen, but that reveals again the power of God's loving self-offer that is always greater than the human potential for refusal.

The liturgy assumes and proclaims that Christ is present in both word and sacrament (as he is present also in the ministers and in the people assembled). Christ is present in his word, says the council, "since it is he himself who speaks when the holy scriptures are read in the Church."[15] Through the limited medium of human speech, the proclamation of

the Scriptures is the living "Word of the Lord" for the
people of God assembled; and though both limited and sinful, the preacher is the mediator of this living word to the
actual life situation of the hearers.

Because the homily is to be understood as an integral
part of the liturgy itself, Geoffrey Wainwright has argued
that the homily therefore shares in the foundational characteristics and purposes of liturgy.[16] The homily, like the
liturgy of which it is an essential part, is *anamnetic*–that is, it
recalls what God has done for us, especially in the saving
deeds of Jesus Christ. The homily shares in the grateful
remembering of the Eucharist itself, a remembering that is
not a mere memory of past events but rather a powerful
recalling of the past as present now in the midst of the
eucharistic community. As the council says: "The ser-
mon...is the proclamation of God's wonderful works in the
history of salvation, which is the mystery of Christ ever
made present and active in us, especially in the celebration
of the liturgy."[17] The liturgical homily is therefore also necessarily and powerfully doxological, leading to thanks and
praise as well as offering an even greater motive for cele-
brating the Eucharist.[18]

## WHAT IS THE CHRISTIAN MORAL LIFE?

If we are to ask how preaching impacts the moral life,
we must have a clear and coherent understanding of the
moral life. For some, the moral life of Christians is fundamentally a matter of obeying rules and fulfilling duties,
whether these rules are derived from the Bible, from
human reason informed by faith, or from church authority.
This deontological (duty-based) view of the Christian moral
life can be held by those who welcome this vision and therefore desire an ever-clearer explication of its consequent
duties for the particular circumstances of life. It can also be

held by those who reject a Christian vision of the moral life altogether precisely because it seems to be a mere proliferation of rules and duties that seem disconnected from the "real" world and their everyday existence within it.

Certainly, rules and laws, obedience and responsible fidelity have an important role to play in the Christian moral life, but to place them first is to form a skewed view of Christian morality. In fact, the moral life of Christians is fundamentally a life of grateful response to God's offer of relationship in Christ. God offers a share in the divine life itself, a share in God's own holiness. The Christian life is a life of discipleship, following Jesus, that involves becoming morally good as the foundation to attaining, by God's grace, the holiness to which God invites us. Moral rules and laws guide us in choosing those actions that are truly in keeping with God's will and that can truly lead us to God. These rules and the duties related to them have an important role to play, but they are secondary to the fundamental sense of the Christian life, both moral and spiritual, as a grateful response to God.

Pope John Paul II begins his 1993 encyclical on the moral life, *Veritatis Splendor,* not with a discussion of law and duty but with an extended reflection on the gospel story of the rich young man who comes to Jesus asking what he must do to attain eternal life.[19] Certainly, in the course of the encyclical, the pope will have a good deal to say about authentic moral rules. The text of the pope's letter, however, suggests strongly that a discussion of rules can be understood best *after* an extended reflection on a young man whose fundamental question involves his search for the authentic path to eternal life and *before* the pope's reflection on the radical commitment of Christian faith manifested in martyrdom. This contextual arrangement of the discussion of morality parallels the placement of the *Catechism's* discussion of morality (Part III) *following* the discussion of the sacraments (Part II) and *before* the discussion of prayer (Part IV).

Without a fundamental sense of Christian morality as a life of grateful response, it is too easy for a legitimate concern for rules, norms, and official moral teaching to sound like a pharisaic concern for the centrality of law. Without a vision of the Christian moral life as grateful response, embraced by those to whom the rules and teaching are addressed, the rules make little sense or are easily dismissed as irrelevant. In this regard, Pope John Paul II quotes St. Augustine, who responds to the question of whether love brings about the keeping of the commandments or if keeping the commandments brings about love by saying: "But who can doubt that love comes first? For the one who does not love has no reason for keeping the commandments."[20]

The moral lives of Christians aim not only at goodness but at holiness. The view of the moral life as fundamentally a matter of following rules misses the basic direction of the Christian life and obscures the relationship of morality and spirituality, moral goodness and authentic holiness. The kinds of actions that Christians perform, the dispositions that they nourish, and the moral character that they seek to build up are grounded in the life of grace, made available in prayer and worship. Christians seek to become good so that, by the grace of God at work in their lives, they can become holy, and their pursuit of holiness empowers and shapes their moral living. Liturgical preaching that truly empowers the moral lives of Christians must direct them ultimately to the holiness that is the final goal of every Christian life.

## HOW DOES LITURGICAL PREACHING FORM THE MORAL LIFE OF CHRISTIANS?

If preaching were basically a matter of instruction and if the Christian moral life were most basically a matter of obeying laws, then the shape of the relationship between preaching and the moral life would be clear. Much of the instructional Catholic preaching of a previous era may well have revealed a presupposition that the moral life involved following carefully explained, explicit moral doctrine. From this perspective, more properly biblical preaching within the context of the liturgy would, at best, be concerned with the biblically-based or biblically-inspired basis for the rules that guide good moral living. It might be said immediately that this response to the question of the relationship of preaching and the moral life is not wrong so much as it is incomplete, as our previous examinations of both preaching and the moral life have already suggested.

In the context of addressing the failure of moral teaching to impact the lives of many Catholics, John Burke suggests that the problem is precisely the absence of preaching that can truly nurture faith as the necessary ground to embracing that teaching:

> I propose that a basic cause of the rejection or ignoring of Catholic moral teaching by so many of "the people in the pews" is due to the fact that the preaching of the "average" Catholic priest has not been geared specifically and consistently to nourishing faith in Jesus Christ as Lord and Savior.
>
> Yet, Catholics can assent to the teaching of the Church, as that teaching is the interpretation of divine revelation, only in so far as they have mature faith.[21]

Walter Brueggemann has made a similar point in suggesting that ultimately preaching

> requires a poet and not a moralist. Because finally church people are like other people; we are not changed by new rules. The deep places in our lives— places of resistance and embrace—are not ultimately reached by instruction. Those places of resistance and embrace are reached only by stories, by images,

metaphors, and phrases that line out the world differ-
ently, apart from our fear and hurt.[22]

The influence of preaching on the moral life of
Christians occurs most importantly at a foundational level, a
level from which decisions and actions flow.[23] *Fulfilled in Your
Hearing* suggests that, though liturgical preaching largely presupposes the faith of the hearers, it seeks also to build up and
shape that faith. Faith involves a "way of seeing or interpreting the world" that influences the way that the hearers will
act in the world. "The preacher," says the bishops' document,
"is a Christian specifically charged with sharing the Christian
vision of the world."[24] In a similar way, but speaking more
generally of the impact of scripture on the moral life of
Christians, Thomas Ogletree suggests that a true encounter
with the biblical text creates a "fusion of horizons" in which
the reader is opened up to a new world of meaning.[25]

By proclaiming the word of God and by manifesting
the power of that word to interpret one's whole life, preaching forms, strengthens, and empowers a distinctively
Christian vision of reality.[26] By bringing to life the scriptures in the ordinary lives of the people of God, preaching
forms in the Christian community a new vision of the
world. Even in the tragic events of life, touched by grace,
the people one encounters are brother and sister, fellow sinners redeemed by Christ, beloved children of God in whom
Christ my Lord himself dwells. We are, first and foremost,
not businesspersons, Americans, nor spouses, but Christians, disciples of Jesus.

If, week after week, effective preaching helps a community to realize that the scriptures illumine the most authentic
meaning of daily living, then preaching cannot but build up
and focus a Christian vision of all of the events and encounters of our daily lives. In this sense, good preaching over time
"trains" disciples to see reality with a vision shaped by the

scriptures and by the paschal mystery, revealed as the key to the most authentic understanding of all of human living. As, Sunday after Sunday, the homilist brings the word of God to shed light on various aspects of daily experience, disciples are subtly but truly formed to see life from the perspective of a faith shaped by the scriptures.[27] In fact, Walter Brueggemann has proposed that all preaching seeks "a poetic construal of an alternative world."[28] Like Ogletree's comment on the encounter with scripture as an invitation to a "fusion of horizons," Brueggemann's notion of a "construal of an alternative world" suggests that preaching promotes, supports, and shapes a religious and moral conversion.

The Christian vision of reality, formed and strengthened and empowered by preaching the word of God, necessarily impacts my attitudes, my decisions, my actions. If the world around me is touched by grace, then surely I must embrace it—both in what brings me joy and sadness. If the people around me are not simply enemies or threats or inconveniences, then how must I act toward them but with generosity, kindness, respect, and reverence? If my very life is a gift, if I am a disciple of Jesus before anything else, if God Almighty has made this sinner both child and friend, then how must I treat my own life, reverence the lives of others like me, and build the priorities of my life and of my daily decisions? If the world around me is a gift that reflects its Creator, charged with God's grandeur, then how shall I treat it except with respect, with awe, in a spirit of responsible stewardship? In sum, as Brueggemann suggests: "The event of preaching is an event in transformed imagination."[29]

To say all of this is to say that preaching forms and strengthens and empowers the life of ongoing conversion, which is the journey upon which every Christian walks from the moment that they accept the gift of faith and are baptized.[30] In fact, in challenging priests to take up their "first task" as ministers of God's word, the council urged them to recall that their fundamental mission was to issue an "urgent invitation...to conversion and holiness."[31] The most basic aim of preaching is the conversion of the whole person, which is certainly moral and profoundly spiritual.

To say that preaching seeks to empower conversion, however, also means that every event of authentic preaching, in which the Christian community encounters the word of God in the actual situations of their lives, is also challenge: Will we accept it? Will we accept the implications of the word for our daily lives, though it runs contrary to the values, expectations, and priorities of the world around us? Although it runs contrary to the affective response we were taught by the secular world, will we act on the challenge of the word to us in this situation—forgive the person who has offended, embrace the person who is different, stand beside the person who is marginalized because he or she is now seen as brother or sister? Can we accept the word that challenges us to share freely the unneeded material things we desire, pursue, and treasure? In the end, preaching seeks conversion rather than coercion, and the hearer remains free to reject the challenge of this encounter with the word of God.

Of course, the goal of preaching is not just personal conversion, but the formation of the community of disciples, the church. As Raymond Brown remarked in a study of preaching in the Acts of the Apostles, the call to repent is quickly followed by a call to be baptized, to enter into *koinonia*. Preaching, therefore, calls the hearers not only to individual conversion and personal holiness but to enter into and to build up the holiness of the people of God.[32] Liturgical preaching, then, not only takes place in the context of a communal celebration; it is directed to building up the community itself, particularly in its central act of worship in the Eucharist.

Moral theologian Bernard Häring maintained that there are two basic forms of the Christian's response to

God: worship (personal and communal) and the moral life. The proclamation of the word of God and its interpretation in the act of preaching announces again the good news of the divine self-offering in Jesus Christ. It demands a response in prayer and in living—a response that is manifest in a special way at the Eucharist, in which the self-offering of Christians is joined with the self-offering of Christ—and a response that is lived out every day in the ordinary encounters, decisions, and relationships that make up the daily lives of Christian men and women.

Häring provides, then, a valuable foundation for understanding the relationship of spirituality and moral living as two interrelated modes of response to God's self-offer in Christ. The response of worship, both personal and communal, empowers the Christian moral life, and good moral living grounds the celebration of the liturgy.[33] Liturgical preaching, as an integral part of the liturgy, seeks to shape both the moral and spiritual lives of its hearers as a response to God who is present in word and sacrament, offering again a share in the divine life.

Is there, then, no room for preaching that addresses specific principles, values, or norms? Does the moral impact of preaching occur only at the foundational level of the formation of a Christian vision and the attitudes that flow from it? Clearly, there is yet an important place for addressing specific moral issues as these are enlightened by the word of God. Certainly the Catholic moral tradition has identified important rules that guide the formation of conscience and the actions of Christians in specific circumstances. Furthermore, there is a place, too, of course, for church doctrine about specific issues, noting how these teachings flow from the scriptures. Some theologians have explained how preaching on moral issues can be done in a way that respects the Lectionary cycle of scriptural readings, which must remain the basis of all liturgical preaching.[34] They have addressed as well the limits of the scriptures to speak to the specifics of particular moral issues and the limits of preaching as a particular kind of discourse within the context of the liturgy.

My purpose, however, is not to address the important question of a method for preaching on particular moral issues. My purpose is more foundational and more urgent: to demonstrate that without sustained preaching that truly forms Christians consistently and effectively over time in their identity as such, both preaching and teaching on specific moral issues will surely fail, no matter how clear or emphatic or often repeated. For people who do not have a Christian vision with its consequent commitments, attitudes, and priorities, any moral rules that flow from Christian faith and that can authentically shape the Christian life will make no sense. The rules will seem naive, or unrealistic, or unrelated to the "real world" in which people live; though, in fact, faith reveals the rules to give direction to an authentic human life. In an age that no longer accepts uncritically everything that comes from authority simply because it is authoritative, how will people accept valid moral norms in questions of sexual morality or medical ethics or about the conduct of business, if they are not first converted to a truly Christian view of life, of other people, and of themselves in that context? Moral preaching about specific issues, outside the context of a sustained history of effective preaching on Christianity identity, is doomed to fail—to be dismissed by those Christians who have taken the name but not the commitment or to be embraced blindly by those who think that following more rules is the essence of Christian living.

Clearly, the New Testament contains moral injunctions concerning appropriate dispositions and actions, but the foundational moral message of the New Testament is directed to a fundamental change of self, of vision, of identity. New Testament authors are clearly concerned with good moral living, but they presuppose that it can only be built on the foundation of a sustained commitment to discipleship, to living in Christ, to accepting the inbreaking of the reign of God. Surely today's Christian preacher will also be concerned with good moral living, but following the logic of the biblical authors and preachers, contemporary homilists must see that the more fundamental challenge is to call Christians truly to embrace the path of discipleship that leads to holiness.

## THE PRIEST AS PRESIDER AND PREACHER OF THE WORD

The council taught that the first duty of the priest is to preach the gospel,[35] a teaching reiterated by Pope John Paul II, who says that the priest "is first of all a *minister of the Word of God.*"[36] To be called to the priesthood, then, is to be called to preach, to bring the biblical word to break open people's lives. The priest as preacher, therefore, has an important and foundational role to play in the moral formation of the people of God, as the reflections above have suggested.

The pope goes on to say that the priest as a minister of the word must develop a deep personal familiarity with the scriptures. "He needs to approach the word," says the pope, "with a docile and prayerful heart, so that it may penetrate his thoughts and feelings and bring about a new outlook in him."[37] As a minister of the word, he must remember that the word is not his, that he is the servant and not the master of the word, and that he is not the sole possessor of the word. Together with a deep personal engagement with the scriptures, he should develop a love for and sensitivity to the tradition of the church and to the official teachings that seek to draw out the implications of the scriptures for the lives of Christians. Far deeper than the study of commentaries and reflection on specific Lectionary texts, good homily preparation is meant to build on this solid ground.

While preaching the word is the first task of the priest, his liturgical ministry of the word points to and is completed in the Eucharist, since the Eucharist is "the source and the summit of all preaching of the Gospel."[38] In his dual role as presider over the community's worship and as preacher of the word, the priest manifests the unity of word and sacrament, which is to be understood as "one single act of worship." It is to be expected, therefore, that the one who presides is generally the one who preaches.[39]

To preside and to preach in the midst of the eucharistic assembly manifests the very identity of the priest as one who represents Christ, the shepherd of his people. Acting most basically in the person of Christ as head and shepherd *(in persona Christi capitis),* the priest calls the people to worship; he proclaims the word as a living word for the actual lives of the people assembled; and he gathers their grateful self-offering to the Father into the self-giving of Christ. Acting, at the same time, in the person of the church *(in persona ecclesiae),* the priest attends to the life situations of the people to be addressed by the word of God; he speaks on behalf of the people their grateful remembering of both word and sacrament; and he presides at worship on their behalf.

As a *preacher,* the priest is a "mediator of meaning," standing between the word of God and the people of God in their everyday life experience, speaking both to and for the people.[40] He does so in the place of Christ whose word is proclaimed and preached (who *is* the Word proclaimed and preached)—a word that demands a response. As a *presider,* the priest stands at the head of the worshiping community, recalling in the church's great Eucharistic Prayer the wonderful history of God's saving deeds, a salvation made present again in the sacramental encounter. In grateful response to both word and sacrament, the assembled disciples offer their lives in return, through the action of the priest, and implicitly but powerfully commit themselves to live in their daily lives the self-giving love of God in Christ encountered anew in the word proclaimed and in the eucharistic communion.

The Eucharist shapes the lives of Christians after the model of the self-giving love of God in Christ made present again in word and sacrament. The moral lives of Christians, therefore, are powerfully and foundationally shaped to realize ultimately the participation in the divine life that they encounter at the Eucharist. In the course of the celebration, the Spirit of God is invoked in the proclamation of the word, in the eucharistic action, and in the sending forth of the assembly to live what they have encountered anew and celebrated (the *epikletic* aspect of both liturgy and of the liturgical homily).[41] The Christian life—as the effort to become one who performs the actions that can be conformed by grace to the pattern of the divine love—is grounded therefore in the Eucharist and points to the Eucharist as the anticipation of its fulfillment. Thus, the priest whose ministry is tied in a special way to the Eucharist has an important role to play in the moral formation of the community even when he is not explicitly speaking about moral issues.

CONCLUSION

To be called to preach the word of God to the people of God, especially within the context of the Eucharist, ought to fill every preacher with a sense of awe, gratitude, and humility. In the event of preaching, the preacher stands between the word of God, of which he is a servant, and the people of God, for whom he is servant-leader after the model of Jesus. He speaks the word of God to the real lives of his brothers and sisters, recognizing that Christ is present in the assembly of the people of God, in the proclamation of the word, in his own life and ministry as a priest, and of course in the eucharistic action itself.[42]

Preaching, therefore, is both a tremendous gift and a tremendous challenge. Certainly as a servant of the word proclaimed, the preacher accepts an obligation to prepare well in study, in prayer, and in reflection—and more basically, in a regular and prayerful encounter with God's word and in loving attention to the people to whom he ministers. If, however, every act of liturgical preaching calls the people of God to an ever deeper conversion and ever more consistent conforming of their lives to the pattern of God's self-giving love manifest in Christ, then in every act of preaching, the preacher accepts the challenge anew to attend to his own conversion.[43] If liturgical preaching seeks to form the lives of its hearers, no less does it seek to form the life of its proclaimer. In fact, to preach in the midst of the community is to accept the challenge to manifest in one's own life the message proclaimed, lest the proclamation be compromised by the inconsistency of the preacher's own life. In the end, the encounter with the living word of God in the act of preaching within the context of the entire liturgy aims at the ongoing conversion of preacher and assembly until their entire lives are taken up perfectly in the divine love of triune life.

## NOTES

1.  Charles Bouchard makes this point in his helpful article, "Authentic Preaching on Moral Issues," *In the Company of Preachers*, eds. Regina Siegfried and Edward Ruane (Collegeville, Minn.: Liturgical Press, 1993), 191.

2.  See Bouchard's article for a general perspective. Walter J. Burghardt focuses on preaching on matters of justice in his *Preaching the Just Word* (New Haven: Yale University Press, 1996).

3.  Catholic Church, National Conference of Catholic

Bishops, Bishops' Committee on Priestly Life and Ministry, *Fulfilled in Your Hearing: The Homily in the Sunday Assembly* (Washington, D.C.: United States Catholic Conference, 1982), 29. (Hereafter, *FIYH*)

4. Catholic Church, *Code of Canon Law*, trans. Canon Law Society of America (Washington, D.C.: Canon Law Society of America, 1983), 768.

5. *FIYH*, 18.

6. *FIYH*, 20. Robert P. Waznak offers a helpful discussion of different images of the preacher within the Catholic tradition, including the preacher as interpreter. See Robert P. Waznak, *An Introduction to the Homily* (Collegeville, Minn.: Liturgical Press, 1998), 47–60.

7. *FIYH*, 7–8.

8. *FIYH*, 10–11.

9. Mary Catherine Hilkert, *Naming Grace: Preaching and the Sacramental Imagination* (New York: Continuum, 1997). I am indebted more broadly to Hilkert's insights into the nature of preaching.

10. Waznak, 54.

11. Note that Hilkert's book is subtitled "Preaching and the Sacramental Imagination."

12. See Frank C. Quinn, "Liturgy: Foundation and Context for Preaching," in *In The Company of Preachers*, 7–25.

13. Catholic Church, Second Vatican Council, *Sacrosanctum Concilium)* (Constitution on the Sacred Liturgy) #52 in *Vatican Council II: The Conciliar and Post Conciliar Documents*, ed. Austin Flannery (Collegeville, Minn.: Liturgical Press, 1975). (Hereafter, *SC)*

14. *SC*, 56, in Flannery, 19.

15. *SC*, 7, in Flannery, 5.

16. Wainwright identifies four characteristics of the liturgy that extend to the liturgical homily: doxological, anamnetic, epikletic, and eschatological. See Geoffrey Wainwright, "Preaching as Worship," *The Greek Orthodox Theological Review* 28 (Winter 1983): 326. Waznak adds a fifth: ecclesial. See Waznak, 20–23.

17. *SC*, 35 in Flannery, 12.

18. Waznak, 20, 36. See also Gerard S. Sloyan, *Worshipful Preaching* (Philadelphia: Fortress Press, 1984), 11–14.

19. Pope John Paul II, *Veritatis Splendor: Regarding Certain Fundamental Questions of the Church's Moral Teaching* (Encyclical Letter, August 6, 1993) (Washington, D.C.: United States Catholic Conference, 1993).

20. Saint Augustine, quoted by Pope John Paul II, *Veritatis Splendor.* #22.

21. John Burke, "Preaching Morality in the Age of Dissent," *The Priest* 47 (February 1991): 31.

22. Walter Brueggemann, *Finally Comes the Poet: Daring Speech for Proclamation* (Minneapolis: Fortress Press, 1989) 109–10.

23. To say that preaching influences the moral life of Christians most powerfully and fundamentally at the level of identity and character from which moral action flows is in keeping with contemporary discussion of the use of scripture in ethics. If the scriptures are not moral treatises and if critical exegesis has shown that the moral injunctions of the Bible cannot be simply applied to contemporary situations, then the impact of scripture in forming the Christian moral life lies at another level. For an excellent critical survey of this discussion, see William C. Spohn, *What Are They Saying About Scripture and Ethics?* rev. ed. (Mahwah, N.J.: Paulist Press, 1995).

24. *FIYH,* 18.

25. Thomas W. Ogletree, *The Use of the Bible in Christian Ethics* (Philadelphia: Fortress Press, 1983), 3–4.

26. *FIYH,* 6: "Through words drawn from the Scriptures, from the Church's theological tradition, and from the personal appropriation of that tradition through study and prayer, the preacher joins himself and the congregation in a common vision."

27. *FIYH,* 7–8.

28. Brueggemann, 6.

29. Brueggemann, 109.

30. See Edward K. Braxton, "Preaching as Food for Thought and Action in the Church," in *A New Look at Preaching,* ed. John Burke (Wilmington, Del.: Michael Glazier, 1983), 85–103.

31.  Second Vatican Council, *Presbyterorum ordinis* (Decree on the Ministry and Life of Priests) #4, in Flannery, 868–69. (Hereafter, *PO*)

32.  Raymond E. Brown, "Preaching in the Acts of the Apostles," in Burke, ed., *A New Look at Preaching*, 69–72. See also Sloyan, 69–71.

33.  For a discussion of the relationship of liturgy and moral living, see Mark O'Keefe, *Becoming Good, Becoming Holy: On the Relationship of Christian Ethics and Spirituality* (Mahwah, N.J.: Paulist Press, 1995), 91–109.

34.  See, for example, the works of Bouchard and Burghardt cited above.

35.  *PO*, 4, in Flannery, 868.

36.  Pope John Paul II, *Pastores Dabo Vobis* (I Will Give You Shepherds: On the Formation of Priests in the Circumstances of the Present Day) (Washington, D.C.: United States Catholic Conference, 1992), 26. (Hereafter, *PDV*) Emphasis in original.

37.  *PDV*, 26. See also *FIYH*, 9–15.

38.  *PO*, 5, in Flannery, 871.

39.  *CSL*, 56.

40.  Ibid.

41.  See Wainwright, 333–36; Waznak, 21.

42.  *SC*, 7, in Flannery, 4–5.

43.  *PDV*, 26.

*Kenneth R. Himes, O.F.M.*

# The Formation of Conscience:
# The Sin of Sloth and the
# Significance of Spirituality

Conscience is at the heart of the moral life. The term *conscience* is, however, famously vague and is often used by people in ways that are not easily reconciled, if not outright contradictory. Yet the word *conscience* remains central to most descriptions of the moral life. In what follows I will highlight one of the connections between the spiritual life and the moral life by showing spirituality's importance for the formation of conscience. First, I will clarify the various meanings of *conscience* and indicate the understanding of conscience that I consider especially important for linking spirituality and morality. Then I will note the threat to the formation of a good conscience by what the tradition has called the capital sin of sloth. In the third part of the paper, I shall suggest how a vibrant spiritual life serves as an antidote to the danger of sloth in the moral life. Finally, I will close with some pastoral implications for the moral formation of people.

## THE MEANINGS OF CONSCIENCE

A difficulty that theologians and philosophers have with the term *conscience* is that in the English language the same word is used to describe diverse yet related aspects of our moral experience. As the Irish moral theologian Sean Fagan has written, "The word 'conscience' has had such a complex, ambiguous history and has been used with so many meanings that it is difficult to confine it to a simple definition."[1] In the classical world, the Greek word *syneidesis,* literally, a "knowing with," was the term used by philosophers to describe "the experience of self-awareness in the forming of moral judgements *[sic]*."[2] Centuries later, in the New Testament, the term had come to mean the ability of human beings to "evaluate the moral worth of their behavior in the light of their beliefs."[3] It was, for Paul, "the moral personality, the centre of the soul where choices are worked out and responsibilities undertaken."[4]

Patristic authors "relied heavily upon Paul, stressing the idea he adopted from Old Testament prophetic literature of a moral law written by God on men's hearts."[5] Jerome, however, introduced a rare Greek term—*synteresis* or *synderesis*—to describe the power of conscience that survived even the Fall. This *synteresis* was understood as the person's inner call to authenticity and pursuit of the human good.

Later medieval theologians who sought "to do justice to both authorities...applied the Pauline term to the actual exercise, or judgment of conscience, while reserving Jerome's term for the idea of conscience as an innate permanent capacity" within each individual.[6] In effect, Jerome's *synteresis* became the human being's intuitive grasp of the first principles of the moral life, while Paul's *syneidesis* was used to designate the practical reasoning ability of a person applying the principles to specific actions.

Over time, as moral theology became focused on the resolution of pastoral problems, various theological authors placed conscience at the center of their ethical theories. Concurrent with this positioning of conscience in moral experience, theologians struggled "to distinguish carefully different states of conscience in view of law and freedom: the firm conscience, the doubtful conscience, the broad conscience, the scrupulous conscience, and so forth."[7]

By the time of the manualists, the experience of conscience was largely described in terms of states pertinent to the process of decision making: (1) true and false conscience; (2) certain and doubtful conscience; (3) perplexed conscience; (4) scrupulous conscience; (5) lax conscience; (6) probable conscience.[8] In order to assist people in sorting through the details of moral decision making, and to enable the person to avoid the pitfalls of conscience formation suggested by some of the categories noted above, an array of moral systems was created. The details of these moral systems need not concern us here, but their role in the formation of conscience was to help an individual determine freedom or obligation relative to a particular precept. We need only note that, by the mid-point of the twentieth century, conscience had come to be largely identified in popular idiom and by many moral theologians with concrete judgments in decision making.[9]

With the renewal of moral theology, we have seen growing interest in retrieval of a richer notion of conscience than simply that of *syneidesis,* a faculty of decision making. A quick survey of commonly used texts within American Catholic moral theology today suggests a fairly popular set of distinctions. Timothy O'Connell has suggested that we understand conscience in three ways, generally corresponding to the traditional categories of *synteresis,* moral science, and *syneidesis.*[10] According to O'Connell, the first understanding of conscience is "as an abiding human *characteristic*,...an awareness of human responsibility.... It is to be a being in charge of one's life," a "human capacity for self-direction."[11] Conscience in the second sense "is the process which that characteristic demands,...the effort to achieve a specific perception of values,...the ongoing process of reflection, discernment, discussion, and analysis."[12] The third sense of conscience described by O'Connell is as "an *event*,....the concrete judgment of a specific person pertaining to her or his own immediate action."[13]

Richard Gula closely follows O'Connell in the description of conscience. Instead of O'Connell's terms—*characteristic, process,* and *event*—to designate the different aspects of conscience, Gula suggests *capacity, process,* and *judgment* but means by the terms the same moral phenomena.[14] Gula emphasizes that he is not talking about "three different realities...but simply the three senses in which we can understand the one reality of conscience."[15]

In her recent volume, which is described as a feminist exploration in Catholic moral theology, Anne Patrick writes, "Conscience is simply a *dimension of the self,* one central to our experience of moral agency." She goes on to say:

> I define it as personal moral awareness, experienced in the course of anticipating future situations and making moral decisions, as well as in the process of reflecting on one's past decisions and the quality of one's character, that is, the sort of person one is becoming.[16]

Here Patrick combines elements of what the tradition called "antecedent" and "consequent" conscience and alludes to the different dimensions of conscience as "moral awareness," the "course of anticipating future situations," and "making moral decisions." These latter expressions would seem roughly to coincide with the threefold framework of O'Connell and Gula.

Lest one conclude that the agenda behind this differentiation of conscience is a liberal or revisionist reading of the tradition, let me cite an influential conservative voice in Catholic moral theology. In the first volume of his multivolume work on Christian morality, philosopher Germain Grisez notes that for Vatican II "conscience refers at once to awareness of principles of morality, to the process of reasoning from principles to conclusions, and to the conclusions, which are moral judgments on choices made or under consideration." He further recalls that Thomas Aquinas used the terms *synteresis* for the sense of conscience as "awareness of principles," *practical reasoning* for "the process of reasoning," and *conscience* for the concluding "moral judgments on choices."[17]

Thus, within the tradition, the one English word *conscience* may allude to different dimensions of moral experience. Whether they use classical or contemporary terminology, recent authors have sought to distinguish the various types of moral experience that are lumped together under the popular designation *conscience*. The purpose of recalling these various aspects of our moral experience and the reason for citing the Catholic tradition's semantics on the topic are to emphasize that we can ignore a central role for spirituality in the moral life if we do not expand the discussion of conscience to include more than decision making. In addition, directing our attention to conscience in the sense of the person's serious search for value, truth, and the good will alert us to a significant pastoral obstacle that stands in the path of moral growth: the vice traditionally called sloth.

## SLOTH AS THE ENEMY OF CONSCIENCE

In the medieval period, there was no settled list of capital sins, although there was considerable redundancy among many lists. Two sins, *tristitia* (melancholy) and *acedia* (apathy), were seen to be closely related, with the former understood as a component of the latter. *Acedia* was a word covering a "jumble of notions" that referred to mental (boredom), spiritual (indifference), moral (apathy), and physical (laziness) states.[18] *Acedia* eventually was translated as "sloth" in English-language lists of the capital sins. Unfortunately, sloth has come to be understood in modern usage as laziness or shiftlessness, missing the other medieval senses of the term beyond the physical. As a result, the real evils that earlier generations of Christians sought to name by the Latin words have slipped into the background.

When used in the moral sense, the person seized by *acedia* is the affect-less individual, one incapable of investment or commitment, a person who cannot get deeply involved in any cause or relationship. Such an individual is unable to take an interest in or to care about things that normally one would. It is this understanding of sloth that I consider to be the real enemy of sound conscience formation. Sloth as moral apathy is what hinders a person from pursuing that which is good. It is a refusal to seek the good because it is difficult and demanding. As one modern writer put it, sloth "is a refusal to be moved, and to be moved especially to any real endeavor, by the contemplation of the good and the beautiful."[19] This way of looking at sloth presumes that the moral agent "has a duty to do more than resist evil; he must also undertake to do good."[20]

The radical evil of sloth can be seen in the way it opposes the theological anthropology that is at the heart of Catholic teaching on conscience. The Catholic understanding of the person is that we are endowed by God with an ability to be self-transcendent; there is within the person a moral summons to be transformed into a more authentic human. Another recent textbook in moral theology describes the full meaning of conscience to be "not just the ability to make decisions about ethical questions confronting us in the present moment," but rather conscience is

> a deep and abiding hunger within us to move beyond ourselves, a moral appetite constantly urging us on beyond all our limits and boundaries, calling us to stretch ourselves beyond our selfish and petty concerns, reaching out for others, for the moral good and ultimately for God.[21]

Conscience as *synteresis* is the moral dimension of the call to self-transcendence. To hear the call of conscience is to be aware of the divine invitation to become more fully and authentically human. At one level, conscience is the call to be an imitator of Christ, since it is Jesus alone who has plumbed the depths of what it means to be human. For the disciple, being truly one's self means being in Christ. Therefore, in seeking to understand the meaning of conscience, we can say that it has to do with our awareness of what it means to become authentically human.

Sloth is a capital sin precisely because we are creatures graced with the capability of growth into a deeper and richer participation in life, and sloth undercuts the drive to self-transcendence. Sloth permits the voice of conscience to be muted so that the moral quest for goodness ceases. An individual's passion for the good dissolves, and the conscience of the slothful person permits self-satisfaction instead of inviting self-transcendence. Those who are morally mature experience a deep attraction for the good, are drawn to it, and fall in love with it; but those who are slothful experience what the biblical writers called "a hardening of the heart," a developing indifference to the good.

## SPIRITUALITY AND THE STRUGGLE AGAINST SLOTH

Sloth as moral apathy requires a diagnosis and remedy that is different from sloth viewed as laziness. When sloth is reduced simply to laziness, the remedy becomes obvious: We ought to work harder. Moral indolence is cured by the discipline of diligent and persistent performance of good deeds. Viewed this way, sloth is something we can control and combat by our own efforts. If, however, sloth is best understood as apathy, as a loss of feeling for the good, then the challenge is of a different kind: We need to care again. If care is absent, however, if we are without passion, lacking a desire for the good, it becomes evident that we cannot correct the problem solely by ourselves. What is needed for the person is to be moved once again, to have passion reawakened. It is in this regard that spirituality becomes important for combating sloth. According to the early monastic tradition, which gave rise to the listing of capital sins, sloth can only be overcome through the indwelling of God. It is by having God move within us that we experience a rebirth of desire and care.

Of course it is not possible to force God's action, to summon God to come into our lives in a new and revivifying way. The early monks knew that truth well. They also thought it possible, however, to engage in various practices that opened up interior space for the Spirit of God to move, for instance, *lectio divina,* contemplation of nature's beauty, and fasting. It is spiritual renewal that rekindles our longing for God, a God whom we may experience as all-caring, concerned, and loving toward oneself, others, and creation.

There are a variety of ways in which a living spirituality counteracts the dangers of sloth. By a living spirituality I mean more than an affect-less acknowledgment of God's existence or a passive recitation of prayers. First and foremost, spirituality entails an encounter with the one who is holy and who is known in the world about us. For Christians, this encounter with God is most clearly experienced in the person of Jesus who reveals a God who is love. Discipleship is an expression of spirituality, our response to this personal God who is revealed in the life of Jesus of Nazareth. We follow Jesus so that we may come to know the living and true God. Seen in this way, the moral life of a believer is but a dimension of discipleship, the grace-empowered response to God's action in the world through Jesus and others.

Thus, Christian morality can never be mere external obedience to a legal norm or abstract ideal. Rather, it must be a response to God that engages the total self, both internal and external. As disciples, we are to love God, not just obey God. As Edward Vacek reminds us, "Love is not only an affirmation. Love also means receiving the beloved into one's self, that is, being affected. God's love of us implies that we make a difference to God. When one embraces, one is also touched."[22] The spirituality of the disciple involves the experience that we matter to God, "that our simplest and most complex strivings" are of significance not only to ourselves but to God. A living spirituality takes us beyond an intellectual acknowledgment that our God is a God of self-offering to an acceptance both intellectual and affective that "we belong to God" (1 Jn 4:6). Such a love transforms us, for we now live with an awareness that our lives are not simply ours alone.[23]

There is a second way that spirituality helps us counteract sloth. Central to a vibrant spiritual life is the practice of prayer that maintains the distinctive tone of moral activity that ought to be characteristic of disciples. As the new Israel, the church has been called into the intimacy with God in Jesus that is recorded in the Gospel of John (e.g., 10:30). For the good to have an appeal that is stronger than the attraction of vice, it is necessary for followers of Jesus to develop a covenantal relationship with God. The offer of covenant is a grace that we do not deserve, but scripture tells us that God freely chose to enter into such a relationship with creation. As a result of the divine initiative, the life of discipleship requires more than conformity to a code of ethics. Personal encounter with the God of Jesus Christ prevents a covenantal morality from becoming a contractual ethic, that is, a legalistic approach to the moral life concerned with not violating rules or commandments. Prayer helps us appreciate that the goal of our moral action is not loyalty to an abstract ideal but a grateful praise of God for what we have received in love.

Through prayer, the believer maintains the proper interior disposition for the moral life. Prayer prevents us from losing sight of God amidst all the preoccupations that fill our lives. Eucharistic rituals, for example, reinforce the dialogic character of life. We are caught up in a blessing of God, a sacrifice of praise for all that God does. The gift-response nature of the moral life is kept before our eyes by participation in such a ritual.

Cultivation of a personal relationship with God avoids the trap of becoming deists in our moral lives, acknowledging some sort of distant responsibility and accountability to an impersonal creator. Rather, Christian morality places all the values and norms of the moral life within the context of a loving and intimate kinship with Jesus and the God he reveals. Spirituality is necessary both *as an aid* to the moral life, permitting the moral response to be an interior one, and *as the fruition* of the moral life, once we realize that nothing we can do adequately responds to divine love, and so we must stand before God in praise and worship.

A third dimension of how spirituality counteracts sloth is seen in the area of motivation. Spirituality empowers us to act in a morally appropriate manner, and this is evident in two ways. On the one hand, we all act out of mixed motives (love, vainglory, desire for reward, fear of punishment, shame, peer and societal pressures, compassion, etc.). Part of moral growth is to examine what it is that encourages us to do the good. A vibrant spirituality helps us to purify our motives, for it encourages us to act out of a desire to respond in love to the love that we experience. Moral action flowing from love must be rooted in ongoing encounters with the God who is love, the God who touches our hearts and fires our spirit. If such moments of prayerful contemplation of God are absent, it becomes far easier for other motives to move to the foreground. When higher motives for morality are diminished and inferior motives predominate, it becomes possible for the believer to gradually lose the desire and longing for the good. It is not likely that lesser motives can sustain the disciple in the struggle against apathy when one faces disappointment and difficulty and the moral life demands sacrifice and suffering.

This leads to the other aspect of motivation in the moral life. Besides purifying our motives, the spiritual life provides a depth of passion and zeal that moves us more powerfully than intellectual appeals to an ideal known only in the abstract. The moral life is not just something cerebral but visceral. Moral action requires a struggle of the will as well as of the mind. To move the will, what is required is not only an appeal to alleged facts but an encounter with Christ. Disciples are not in love with "truth" or the "good"—they are in love with a personal God who is truth and goodness.

Meditation on the gospels, participation in sacramental rites, and individual and group devotions are ways in which we come to know Jesus. By knowing Jesus experientially, we can be inspired by him, fired with love to follow him, and serve him. Oftentimes it does little good for us to tell ourselves to stop our participation in a destructive lifestyle, to "just say no." We need to reorient ourselves to a new source of energy, something that moves us, draws us in the direction of the good despite the appeal of vice. We must find something to which we can devote ourselves. Prayer, understood broadly as attending to God, helps us to do that, to fall in love with God. Liturgical symbols, hymnody, good preaching—all have the power to evoke a response that is affective and compelling.

Prayer and other elements of the spiritual life can school our emotions so that we are drawn to the good, while also providing us with emotional energy to seek and choose the good, despite obstacles and suffering. Unless we love the good, unless we care about the morally right thing to do, it is hard to imagine that we will be able to sustain the life of discipleship. Sloth deadens the passions and leads us to indifference to the good. A life marked by regular practices of personal prayer and frequent participation in the liturgical life of a community offers an antidote to sloth, since it will be a life in which we are taught to care deeply about the good, for we know the good experientially as it is found in the living God.

In sum, the formation of a Christian conscience must entail not merely tools for clear thinking but also the training of our passions, so that we truly desire the good and want to do what is right. Spirituality is instrumental in this process, for conscience must integrate both cognitive and affective dimensions of human personality.[24]

## THE FORMATION OF CONSCIENCE

In the present state of Roman Catholic teaching, the dignity of conscience is held as the highest personal norm. At Vatican II the bishops proclaimed that "conscience is the most secret core and sanctuary" of a person. To listen to one's conscience and follow it "is the very dignity" of the person. The bishops' emphasis on the primary importance of conscience is such that they acknowledge that a conscience may be in error "from invincible ignorance without losing its dignity."[25] To make sense of this latter statement, we must remember that "appeal to conscience as a moral authority for one's actions presupposes a 'good conscience.'"[26] That is, the conciliar teaching presumes that synteresis, conscience as inner call to moral responsibility, is what each person must follow. We must pursue the good as we see it. Provided that we have made an honest effort to learn what we can about the matter under review, we are bound to follow our conscience. This is so even if others see my action to be wrong. As long as I do not know it to be wrong, but believe myself to be right, I must follow the truth as it speaks to me in the sanctuary of conscience. Being faithful to the truth, as best I can know it, is the measure of being in good conscience.

The distinction between the pairs of words "good/bad" and "right/wrong" is a familiar one to Catholic moral theologians. Good/bad refers to *synteresis,* and as long as one is acting in good conscience, one is not morally blameworthy even if one is wrong at the level of conscience as *syneidesis.* People may sincerely search for the good while not always making right decisions. Honest mistakes do occur. Hence, we see the wisdom of Anne Patrick's observation that conscience is not some sort of moral radar, always honing in on the correct judgment. Rather, it is more like intelligence—we all have some of it; we all could use more of it; and even a lot of it does not mean we are always right.[27] Disciples can make wrong decisions *(syneidesis)* without being dishonest or insincere in their quest for the good *(synteresis).*

Even as the conciliar teaching makes clear, however, the supremacy of conscience can be challenged when a person "who cares but little for truth and goodness" is in error. It is this aspect of the council's teaching I am concerned with in this paper. Generally, it has received less attention than the conciliar teaching that correctly exalts the dignity of conscience. That high view of conscience was a needed clarification about the Catholic teaching, since the church has not always been seen in the modern era as a protector of the freedom of conscience. Yet, the situation today suggests that we must remember: "[E]mphasis on the freedom of conscience and the right and obligation to *follow* it should not blur the fact that there is an equal obligation to *form one's conscience*."[28]

The reason moral theology distinguishes among the various meanings of conscience is not only for the purpose of linguistic precision. Depending on what one means by conscience, there are diverse approaches to what is involved in the formation of conscience. In some cases, for example, conscience as practical judgment, the emphasis will be on *informing* the conscience, acquiring the necessary knowledge in order to make wise judgments. Often when teachers and pastors speak about the need for people to have an informed conscience before making moral choices, it is the attainment of information that they have in mind. One should know what the church teaches about a particular issue, what reliable information from scholarly disciplines about it is available, how this issue impacts human well-being, and so on. In this context, the contribution of spirituality to conscience is akin to learning methods of discernment. That is, spirituality's contribution in this example is largely limited to helping us decide wisely. The dimension of conscience that is pastorally most problematic is not the need people have for information. In our information-rich culture, all sorts of information are abundantly available.

Unfortunately, much of the information to which we have access in American society is misleading and even false; it is presented without context, overhyped, irrelevant to human well-being, and peripheral to our experience. Thus, the task of separating wheat from chaff is as important as ever. Indeed, the wise person in the future will not be the person with the ability to access information but the individual with the skill to screen out and filter information. I wish to argue, however, that what is presumed by those who advocate an *informed* conscience is instead an adequately formed conscience, that is, a conscience that has been motivated and trained to desire the good so that the person will work at being informed.

## PASTORAL IMPLICATIONS

A pastoral problem for our age is that we readily assume the fact of good conscience. Those who have worried about informing conscience have stressed knowing right and wrong, developing prudence and skills in decision making, without taking sufficient note of the duty to form one's conscience. A corollary of viewing conscience mainly as *syneidesis* is to see the human person as a problem solver. The valued traits then become analytic reasoning, rational discourse, disinterested judgment. Other qualities—imagination, openness, creativity, passion, self-criticism, compassion—may be undervalued in such a framework. We have seen this skewed approach in the mistaken operational assumptions of social scientists, for instance, who act as if the best way to observe moral growth is to assess people's judgments in hypothetical cases. Precisely because they are hypothetical, such exercises are of limited value. They remove us from actual involvement in a situation; our answers do not reveal anything about what we would really do or even actually think in real life.

Pastorally, the much needed task is to help each other love the God who is Good. Therefore, at the pastoral level, we may misplace our energies if we focus too much on the conscientious person as decision maker. What is needed today is a renewed interest in the conscientious person as the sincere seeker of truth and the consequent pastoral strategy of evoking passion for the good by schooling people in practices of prayer, both personal and communal.

We need to deepen and transform our desires, to train our affections to love properly. Only if that is done well will we avoid the apathy that stunts the moral quest and makes talk of good conscience doubtful. I would like, then, to suggest a couple of the pastoral implications of the argument that sloth is the enemy of good conscience and that spirituality is the needed counterforce to foster growth in the moral life of the disciple.

Before doing so, let me be clear that I am aware our job as a church is not completed by creating a love for moral goodness, as important as that is. We must also sharpen our ability to make moral judgments that are correct, to become not just people who love, but people who love well. As I have made clear, however, we have spent much time and effort in recent years dealing with conscience and right decision making. Indeed we have so focused on *informing* the conscience, stressing knowledge of right from wrong, that we have paid inadequate attention to *forming* the conscience, of desiring the good and shunning the bad. As a church we have presumed that people were sufficiently zealous and in love with the good so that the processes of prudent discernment would be practiced. Yet, too often the moral difficulty is not lack of knowledge, for we know what it is we should do; the real difficulty is doing the right thing and, even more profoundly, wanting to do it.[29] Having the capacity to reason to correct moral judgments is insufficient if we lack any real commitment to seek and do the good. So I underscore two pastoral implications of my viewpoint.

First, people can come to learn that the morally good life is both possible and attractive. Thus, stories of exemplary figures are worth reading; news accounts of heroic activity should be highlighted and exposure to admirable persons sought. What people need, in part, are standards of heroism, examples of compassion, experiences that challenge their taken-for-granted world of self-interest.

The community of believers must hold up the lives of ordinary persons who display a quiet heroism in the way they live out their commitments, care for their neighbors, and struggle to maintain personal integrity. At the same time, biographies of figures such as Dorothy Day, Thomas More, Bartolomé de Las Casas, Pierre Toussaint, Joan of Arc, Oscar Romero, Francis of Assisi, Mother Theresa, and Thea Bowman are examples of well-known persons whose witness can inspire and guide Christians in their moral growth. The community of faith needs to instill in believers a desire to do the good and to assist disciples in becoming more attuned to the nature of the good life. The goal is to facilitate persons' commitments to be faithful in seeking out the good.

Our moral experience can find us in tension between our sense of ourselves and a life that does not live up to that self-image. A possible reaction is to be spurred into action so as to close the gap between the reality and the moral ideal, for example, being a good parent, teacher, friend, and the like. A properly formed conscience drives us to bring our self-understanding into accord with professed ideals. The incorrect solution for the apathetic, however, is to revise our ideals downward. A conscience captivated by sloth will allow us to avoid the moral tension of conversion by ignoring the call to embrace the good or by convincing us that the moral ideal to which we aspire is too demanding. Seeking the good, loving the good, encourages transformation of the self, such that persons are encouraged to live up to ideals rather than surrender them.

As a community of faith, we need to instill in people a love for goodness, encourage in them a sense of moral idealism whereby they do not succumb to skepticism or cynicism about moral values. Young people especially need to know adults who are committed to excellence in the moral life in the same way that skilled workers are dedicated to excellence in their craft, athletes are committed to excellence in performance of their sport, or musicians devoted to their music.

Second, in considering conscience as an inner call to authenticity and diligence in pursuing the good, an important formative task is to awaken and sharpen moral sensitivity. We respond only to what we experience, to what enters into our consciousness. Too often people who are insufficiently sensitive to moral values do not even grasp the moral dimensions of an experience. How often have we seen a person not even realize how his or her words or actions cause another person's pain? How often do people fail to see what is really at stake in a decision, unable to focus on anything but what is of immediate and direct satisfaction? This is a deficiency in moral sensitivity. It is not that some individuals consciously choose poorly; instead, they are not even capable of grasping all that is embedded in the experience to which they are being asked to respond.

In order to sharpen and deepen sensitivity, a variety of elements can be utilized. Largely these will focus on the affective dimensions of moral growth, for what is at stake is the inability to feel people's pain, the discipline to delay immediate gratification for a higher purpose, the courage to withstand the pressure of peers or societal expectations. Iris Murdoch writes of the grave need to discipline what she calls the "fat relentless ego" and the moral struggle involved in that effort.[30] Sloth always tempts us to complacency in the moral life. It is much easier to remain within a world that does not challenge us to change, that shields us from those who are different from us, a world that allows us to create self-deceiving myths about moral goods and evils. Calling disciples to sacrifice, to sharing their talents and possessions, to working cooperatively, to denying themselves for the sake of another, to working with persistence and care on a project that has only future rewards, to living up to promises—all these are disciplines that restrain the ego and make room for moral growth.

Developing sensitivity is also facilitated by expanding our range of experiences, since in this culture it is relatively easy for many to insulate themselves from what is unpleasant or unrewarding. In more affluent suburban areas, for instance, many people are shielded from the sufferings of the economically deprived. Service projects that introduce us to people in need can awaken feelings of compassion. In many of our homes and neighborhoods, children may not frequently encounter examples of gentleness, patience, or caring. Barraged by larger than life images of sports figures, gun-toting super-heroes, and slick entrepreneurs, the search for true moral examples can be difficult in this culture.[31]

## CONCLUSION

My aim in this essay has been to stress an obligation that might be called *forming* rather than *informing* conscience. In meeting this obligation, there is a significant role for spirituality, since the first task of conscience formation is to teach people a love, even a passion, for the good. Only then can we move to the aspect of conscience that is concerned with making wise and prudent decisions. Looking at conscience formation, as I have used the expression, the major obstacle is sloth, a moral apathy, which permits one to be complacent about rather than passionate for the good. Spirituality's contribution to the formation of conscience as synteresis is to deepen our love, our desire, for the God who is Goodness.

## NOTES

1. Sean Fagan, "Conscience," *The New Dictionary of Catholic Theology*, eds. J. Komonchak, M. Collins, and D. Lane (Wilmington, Del.: Michael Glazier, 1987), 226.

2. John Mahoney, *The Making of Moral Theology: A Study of the Roman Catholic Tradition* (New York: Clarendon Press, 1987), 185.

3. Mahoney, 187.

4. Mahoney 187–88, quoting Philippe Delhaye, *The Christian Conscience* (New York: Desclee, 1968), 42.

5. Mahoney, 186.

6. Mahoney, 187.

7. Servais Pinckaers, *The Sources of Christian Ethics* (Washington, D.C.: Catholic University of America Press, 1995), 272.

8. See, for example, Henry Davis, *Moral and Pastoral Theology*, vol. 1 (London: Sheed and Ward, 1935), 65–80.

9. In such a framework, it was not easy to see the role or significance of spirituality for the moral life. Indeed, prayer often was treated as one more legal obligation that might bind a person, and the same sort of moral calculus used for resolving the force of a law in other areas of life was employed when discussing the legal obligations relevant to the spiritual life.

10. Timothy O'Connell, *Principles for a Catholic Morality*, rev. ed. (San Francisco: Harper & Row, 1990), 109.

11. O'Connell, 110 (emphasis in original unless noted otherwise).

12. O'Connell, 111.

13. O'Connell, 112.

14. Richard Gula, *Reason Informed by Faith* (Mahwah, N.J.: Paulist Press, 1989), 132.

15. Gula, 131.

16. Anne Patrick, *Liberating Conscience: Feminist Explorations in Catholic Moral Theology* (New York: Continuum, 1996), 35.

17. Germain Grisez, *The Way of the Lord Jesus*, vol. 1 (Chicago: Franciscan Herald Press, 1983), 76.

18. Stanford Lyman, *The Seven Deadly Sins: Society and Evil* (New York: St. Martin's Press, 1978), 5.

19. Henry Fairlie, *The Seven Deadly Sins Today* (Washington, D.C.: New Republic Books, 1978), 126.

20. Lyman, 9.

21. Russell Connors, Jr., and Patrick McCormick, *Character, Choices and Community: The Three Faces of Christian Ethics* (Mahwah, N.J.: Paulist Press, 1998), 137.

22. Edward Vacek, *Love, Human and Divine: The Heart of Christian Ethics* (Washington, D.C.: Georgetown University Press, 1994), 123.

23. Vacek, 127.

24. There are other aspects of the relationship between morality and spirituality that could be explored, for example, the role of discernment in decision making or the way images of God shape our moral attitudes. I only wish to suggest here that there is a clear contribution that spirituality makes to the formation of conscience once we consider conscience as more than a faculty for practical moral judgment. Concerning discernment see John Haughey, "The Role of Prayer in Action/Reflection Groups" in *Tracing the Spirit*, ed. James Hug (Mahwah, N.J.: Paulist Press, 1983), 103–21. For the moral import of our images of God, see James Gustafson, "Spiritual Life and Moral Life" in *Theology and Christian Ethics* (Philadelphia: Pilgrim Press, 1974), 161–76.

25. Catholic Church, Vatican Council II, *Gaudium et Spes* (Pastoral Constitution on the Church in the Modern World), 16. See, for example, Austin Flannery, ed., *Vatican Council II: The Conciliar and Post Conciliar Documents* (Wilmington, Del.: Scholarly Resources, 1975).

26. Fagan, in Komonchak et al., 229.

27. Patrick, 35.

28. Fagan, in Komonchak et al., 228.

29. As has been pointed out in a recent text, the danger is that without a desire to seek conscientiously for the good we become "moral 'couch potatoes.'" See Connors and McCormick, 135.

30. Iris Murdoch, *The Sovereignty of Good* (London: Routledge and Kegan Paul, 1970), 52.

31. There are, of course, many other implications that could be drawn out, but I have not done so in the interest of space. One obvious point to be developed is the importance of communal prayer and the celebration of the sacraments for conscience formation. Patricia Lamoureux has explored in a thoughtful way the import of communal celebration of the Liturgy of the Hours for morality. In particular, she discusses the moral vision and virtue of solidarity as developed through such prayer. See "Liturgy of the Hours and the Moral Life," *New Theology Review* 10 (February 1997): 40–57. Timothy O'Connell's new book has several important insights for the topic of sacramental celebration and morality, especially his comments on gesture, music, and the simple fact of being gathered with others. See *Making Disciples: A Handbook of Christian Formation* (New York: Crossroad Publishing, 1998), esp. chs. 11 and 13.

*Edward C. Vacek, S.J.*

# Gifts, God, Generosity, and Gratitude

Gratitude[1] to God is essential to Christian life. James Gustafson, current godfather to so many ethicists in the United States, observes, "Gratitude to God is a fundamental reason for being moral in Judaism and Christianity."[2] Scripture scholar John Koenig goes further when he writes, "It is no exaggeration to claim that this wondrous spiral of grace descending and thanks ascending forms the very axis of Christian faith."[3] Similarly, Brian Childs, writing from a pastoral perspective, asserts that "gratitude, as the truly appropriate and comprehensive response to God's grace in Jesus Christ, is the fundamental orientation for Christian life, the basic motive and perspective for all true worship and faithful living."[4] Catholic ethicist Richard Gula chimes in that gratitude is "the pivotal virtue of the moral life."[5] Thus, for many Christians, gratitude is not only important, not only essential, but the center of the Christian life.

It is surprising, then, that so few theologians have seriously analyzed the meaning of gratitude to God. The topic is by no means simple or uncontroversial. Near the end of an excellent essay on gratitude within human relationships,

Paul Camenisch observed that the ordinary meaning of gratitude does *not* readily apply in relation to God.[6] As we will see, similar problems arise for generosity, both God's generosity to us and our generosity to God.

In several articles and a lengthy book, I have extensively examined the virtue of love.[7] Here I want more briefly to examine two lesser virtues, generosity and gratitude, that derive from love. I hope to show that generosity is best understood through the "excess" that love inspires. Furthermore, I hope to show that, contrary to the authors cited above, gratitude not only is *not* the center of Christian life, but can be inimical to it. Still, when informed by love, gratitude holds an important place in Christian life.

## THREE KINDS OF DIVINE LOVE FOR US

God is good to us. Why? According to the scriptures, sometimes God blesses us for our sake (Ex 18:8; Jos 23:3; 2 Sm 5:12); other times God blesses us not for our sake but for God's own sake (Ez 36:22; Is 48:9–11; Ps 6:4, 23:3, 44:26, 106:8); and at still other times God blesses us both for God's sake and our sake as covenant members (Is 37:35). In my own terminology, God manifests, respectively, "*agape*-love," "*eros*-love," and "*philia*-love."[8]

Agape refers to the love we have for someone quite apart from any gain that might accrue to us.[9] An "agapic" lover is one-sidedly generous, wanting to benefit another, without aiming to receive anything in return. Agapic givers ignore or downplay the costs to themselves. Professionals often exhibit this kind of love in their service.[10]

When God loves us "agapically," God manifests no need or desire for anything from us. God blesses Israel for Abraham's sake (Gn 26:24), for Joseph's sake (Gn 39:5), for David's sake (2 Kgs 8:19), and for Israel's own sake (Ex 18:8). Above all, God so loves the world that God gives

God's own son for the sake of our salvation (Jn 3:16). Out of abundance, the agapic God rescues us and promotes our flourishing; and, thus, as far as we are concerned, God acts "anthropocentrically."

The God of the Bible and of piety is not a purely agapic lover. In our anthropocentric age, where we repeat almost as a mantra that God unconditionally loves us and is devoted to our fulfillment and that, therefore, we too should love ourselves and be devoted to our fulfillment, we easily forget an earlier and more pervasive Christian view: God is the Lord and center of everything and we exist to give glory to God. That is, we are created to praise, reverence, and serve God, a statement that not only tells us what we must do but also implies that we are created for God's sake. This earlier view asserts that God loves us, but loves us with eros, that is, for God's own sake.[11]

*Eros,* of course, is not a standard biblical or theological word for love, but the idea of *eros* is common. For example, throughout the scriptures, we are encouraged to love God by a promise of a hundredfold here and heaven hereafter (Mt 19:29). *Eros* also describes God's love for us. Our God is a jealous God (Jos 24:19). God is at work in us for God's good pleasure (Phil 2:13). We are God's "treasured possession" on whom God "has set his heart" (Dt 7:7). God makes us a people "for himself," and God helps us "for his great name's sake" (1 Sm 12:22). The biblical God affirms and fosters our lives, but only on condition that we render due obedience to God (Dt 30:8–11). In a word, God acts "theocentrically." The psalmist even appeals to God's self-interest in praise as a reason for rescue (Ps 30:9).

*Philia* is the kind of love in which members affectively affirm one another as participants in a common life together.[12] In this mutual relationship, open-ended trust, not rights or duties, prevails. The relationship weakens if any member acts selfishly, demands certain responses, slackens in generosity, or fails to respond gratefully.[13] The members exchange gifts not on demand but willingly, out of a sense of the "grace" of the relationship. Within limits, each member is free to decide whatever, whenever, and however to give and to respond, but all want to do so.

God is also involved with humans in *philia*.[14] We have many expressions to name this love relationship: God makes a covenant with us, dwells among us, and desires to become friends with us. God gives an abundance of gifts to us as members of this relationship and for the benefit of the relationship itself (Jn 3:16, 17:22–23; 1 Jn 4:8–10; Phil 2:6–8). This relationship brings glory to God, not as God's primary motive but as a collateral result (1 Chr 29:12–13; Ps 50:15; Is 26:15; Jn 15:8; 2 Cor 4:15). In a *philia* relationship, God and humans act "theanthropically."

As in relations among humans, so in God's relation to us, these three forms of love are intermingled. As an "agapist," God creates generously and without the goal of getting some return. As an erotic lover, God is the center of the universe, and God blesses, rewards, or forgives in accord with what brings glory to God's own self. As one who participates in a mutual love with us, God sanctifies us, enabling us to share life with God. In the Christian dispensation, *philia*, or friendship with God, is the origin and goal of Christian life as well as the proper context for the other two loves.[15]

## GIFT

Aquinas observed that "love has the nature of a first gift, through which all free gifts are given."[16] Having reflected on love, I now want to ask what a "gift" is. Both generosity and gratitude revolve around the offering of a gift.

The practice of gift-giving varies according to culture. Scholars observe that in many non-Western cultures a "gift" often functions as a mechanism by which a donor controls or obligates a beneficiary. Gifts remain in some sense the property of the "big man" who gives, and so the gift or its equivalent must eventually be returned, often with interest. Gift-giving thus serves to establish and sustain a dominance-submission relationship.[17] Powerful figures give gifts to whomever they choose, and they do so in order to render others indebted, "to ensure a return of honor," and "to ensure continued exact compliance with what has been laid down."[18] The gifts of the sovereign God, as depicted in Judeo-Christian tradition, not infrequently function in these ways. The sovereign Lord gives whatever, whenever, however, and to whomever God chooses (Ex 33:19). This God then demands specific responses from the beneficiaries. They do not own the gifts they have been given. If they are obedient, they will receive more gifts; if not, they will lose what they have already received (Dt 11:13–17; Jer 3:3; Mt 25:28–30). One source of difficulty for a contemporary theology of gift, then, is that this ancient sense of gift is so different from our own.

For us, a gift, roughly speaking, is an "unearned benefit." Stated more fully and exactly, a gift is (1) some value or good deliberately and freely bestowed by a donor (2) primarily to benefit a recipient who has not earned it and who freely accepts it as a gift; this donation (3) initiates or, more commonly, expresses and contributes to a relationship between the donor and recipient; this relationship includes, on the one hand, (4) socially regulated donor obligations concerning giving the benefit, receiving any response, and being a member of the relationship as well as, on the other hand, (5) socially regulated recipient obligations toward the donor, the gift, and the relationship.[19]

This fuller, more academic description of a gift refers to the paradigmatic case. One can easily find counter-examples or borderline cases that do not fit.[20] For example, if my blood donation is not used, have I made a gift? If a Jehovah Witness received the blood, but did not want or does not acknowledge it, has there been a gift?[21] Inversely, people may not intend to give us a gift, and yet we may gladly welcome some "unearned benefit" from them. As an extreme example, our boss might berate us for our faults, and we may, after settling down, be grateful for the truth we have received. Or, more broadly, we receive many of life's goods from people who have no intention of giving us a gift but who are acting simply out of duty or for their own gain. All these nonstandard cases might be thought of as gifts in a broad sense, and thus they illustrate the looseness of the concept.[22] Christians, who are encouraged to see everything as gift (Eph 5:20), incline toward using gift-language very broadly.[23] They speak, for example, about a "gift" of self, of wisdom, of a kidney, of a few more years, of celibacy, of children, or even of suffering and death.

Giving and receiving gifts is important in human life as a way of incarnating the "excess" that love inspires. God so loved the world that God gave up Jesus for our sakes (Jn 3:16) and accordingly will give us everything else too (Rm 8:32). In other words, God gives in excess, as does Jesus when he feeds thousands and still has lots left over (Mk 6:30–44, 8:1–9). Much as the woman at Bethany poured out expensive ointment on Jesus' head (Mk 14:4), so too our impulse to be excessive for those we love follows the same logic of love. When Christians' hearts are overflowing with love, they give not only according to their means but also beyond their means (2 Cor 8:2–5). Having briefly looked at the nature of a gift, let me now move on to analyze the virtues that give rise to gift-giving—generosity and gratitude.

## GENEROSITY

Why are we not more generous? There are, of course, many reasons, but a few cultural obstacles should be pointed out.

*Obstacles*

Can we be generous? No—at least not if we accept a common theme prominent in contemporary psychology and economics. Many psychologists hold that all action is motivated by self-interest. They produce substantial psychological research to prove that we are all necessarily egoists. That is, we always act for our own self-interest, and we never act on behalf of others except as a strategy to promote our own interests.[24] Similarly, many economists propose that the only rational action is one done out of self-interest. For them, human interactions can best be understood as so many contracts made to advance our own well-being.[25] Society itself is described as a social contract we make with one another in order to get for ourselves various goods and services. Thus, according to both of these approaches, apparently generous acts are really long-term strategies for greater personal gain.

A variation of this emphasis on self-interest appears among many contemporary Christians for whom the first great commandment is to love one's own self. They value service to others, of course, but they do so because they get so much out of helping others. Similarly, when they strive to love God, they do so in order to attain their own ultimate happiness.[26] These are not generous motives. Another obstacle to generosity is the recent claim that people have to love themselves before they can love others. Since self-love is a lifelong, never-ending project, generosity is like a rain check that never gets used.

Finally, there is a new social ideology that discourages our generosity. "Charity," which used to be a synonym for generosity, has become a suspect activity. Giving without expecting a return is said to create a culture of dependence, and so being generous to the needy is judged to be wrong.[27]

*Some Characteristics of Generosity*

What is generosity? Like the word *gift, generosity* is a loose term. It is a "more or less" quality. Generosity is determined by (1) size, (2) benefits, (3) supererogation, (4) conditions, (5) intention, (6) costs, and (7) affections.

1. *Size of Gift:* Though generosity is chiefly a virtue of the donor, we also use the word generous to describe the gift itself. It names some benefit that is greater than is normally the case. Thus a restaurant might offer "generous" portions, even though its intention is purely mercenary. Similarly, four dollars is a generous tip for a cup of coffee, even if the wealthy patron was just too busy to wait for change from a five dollar bill.

2. *Benefit:* The gift must, of course, be a real and appropriate benefit. What counts as a benefit is relative to the recipient. Half a loaf of bread likely is a great benefit for a fellow inmate in a Nazi prison camp but not for the owner of a bakery. As we shall see, when we speak of God's generosity, we often focus rather strongly on the greatness of the gift relative to our own neediness.

Of course, some gifts, even when given with good intentions, are not appropriate or upright benefits. An expensive bottle of single-malt scotch given to an alcoholic is no real benefit. The teacher who gives a student an undeserved "A" so that he can continue to play college football may help that student along the path to a lucrative and much desired professional football career, but this is a gift that ought not be given. In other words, there are legitimate constraints on gift-giving.

3. *Beyond Due:* Although there are limits, an act of generosity ordinarily implies giving beyond what is due. Jesus, though only a wedding guest at Cana, went beyond bounds

to create 140 gallons of wine (Jn 2:1–11). If the original supplier had provided twice as much wine, however, but did so only to fill exactly a catering contract, that merchant would not be acting generously.

The criterion of "beyond what is due" sometimes amounts to "beyond what normally occurs" among human beings. For example, people generally are deserving of praise for various good characteristics and actions. Ordinarily, however, people are not inclined to look especially hard for what is praiseworthy in others. Some people, however, are generous with their praise or in their thoughts about others. Such people have a generous spirit.

4. *Conditioned:* In evaluating whether an act is generous, we also consider any implied or expressed conditions associated with the gift. Conditions may indicate whether the donor's intention is benevolent, or they may determine whether the gift is a real benefit. Ordinarily, of course, the conditions are fairly obvious and need not be specified. A baseball bat given as a birthday present is for playing ball and not for hitting one's little sister. Gifts, however, often come with explicit conditions or stipulations. Such conditions may open up new possibilities, but they may also limit the recipient's freedom or even misdirect it. A wealthy man's gift of a hundred thousand dollars to his alma matter is a generous gift even when he specifies that it can only be used for minority student scholarships. This is a real benefit. But his gift should surely be refused if he gives money on the condition that no minority student ever live in his former dorm room. That is not a benefit. The conditions on a gift must free recipients to maintain and expand their own appropriate goals, not coerce or dehumanize them.[28]

5. *Intention:* Ordinarily, for an act to be generous, the dominant motive must be to benefit the recipient. A person

who gives gifts solely to get a return is not generous. In Seneca's quaint comment, "Such a man is like one who provides fodder for his cattle."[29] Still, mixed motives are quite common. A generous gift may also benefit the donor. As Seneca continued, "If he has joined his interests to mine, if he is thinking of both of us, then should I fail to be glad that what was to my advantage was also to his, I would be ungrateful and unjust. To count as a favor only what makes the giver the loser is the worst sort of maliciousness."[30] Hence, if we make a large donation to our parish primarily because we believe in sharing, but also because we need the tax deduction, we are acting generously, though not purely so.

6. *Costly:* Generosity is usually measured in part by how valuable or costly a gift is for the donor.[31] We are not really generous if, just as we are headed to the trash with a pair of old skis, we accede to a neighbor boy's request for them.[32] When we endure some cost in giving, we indicate that the recipient's interests count in some respects more than our own. Jesus praised the widow who gave her small mite, even though her gift was not generous in size or greatly beneficial to someone in need. But her generosity was enormous since she gave all she had. Others gave more, but their gift was less costly for them and therefore less praiseworthy (Lk 21:1–4).

We saw above that sometimes the criterion of "beyond what is due" amounts to "beyond what normally occurs." Similarly, sometimes the criterion of "costliness" amounts to "beyond the costs that most of us ordinarily would experience." If we usually find something good to say about other human beings, our generosity of spirit probably brings pleasure to us and is hardly costly. Still, the fact that most people do not engage in such activities presumably means that for them it would be costly to consistently speak well about someone other than themselves.

7. *Glad Desire:* Thus, talk of costliness should not imply that a generous person gives with a heavy heart. Rather, a benefit is generously given only if it is offered out of glad desire.[33] Moreover, our pleasure must come from the giving and not from some extrinsic source. If we give only with the desire to gain approval or to imitate others who are generous, we are not yet acting with a generous heart.[34] Generosity refers primarily to a certain largess of spirit, and it is a matter of appropriate affections. People for whom an act of kindness goes against their grain are less generous than those whose lives abound with kindness, for "God loves a cheerful giver" (2 Cor 9:7).

### Moral Responsibility to Be Generous

Must we be generous? When the ideology of self-interested individualism reigns, there is a temptation to think that we can do whatever we want, as long as we do not hurt others. I want to argue, however, that we are required to be generous. The chief source of this moral requirement is our responsibility to grow in love.

Most of us praise generosity when we see it. As a virtue, generosity is an excellence in one aspect of a good human life. We consider stinginess to be a vice, a failure in being human. But what about a life that, so to speak, never descends to this vice, but also never ascends to generosity? Would a person who only and always acted justly, giving people their due and nothing more, be living morally?

A life that practiced strict justice would still be far beyond what most of us actually do! Nevertheless, human life requires more than unfailingly just acts; it requires growth in virtue. As Teilhard de Chardin argued,[35] moral living requires us progressively to move beyond an established identity and beyond well-defined relationships. The Christian who says that she chooses not to grow any further in her relationship to God or to her fellow human beings is a person who in fact is deteriorating as a Christian and as a human being.[36]

We are lovers by nature. Love affirms what the beloved is but also inspires us to help the beloved flourish.[37] Love goes beyond bounds; it happily tends to excess. To give to a friend or spouse only what they deserve is to deny the movement of love that constitutes the relationship. From time to time, we must even treat strangers with largess, opening ourselves up to the possibility that they will come to mean more to us. In other words, as "lovers," we must at least occasionally give beyond what is due. The alternative to this generosity is to wither and shrink in spirit.

Yet there is a difficulty with this kind of thinking: How can we have a moral responsibility to be generous, when, as we saw above, generosity means to go beyond what is obligatory? First, our responsibility to become generous is the sort of responsibility that attends to many virtues. We must grow in virtues, but we do not have to be growing in a particular virtue on each and every occasion. We are free, broadly speaking, to choose the occasion in accord with the time, place, person, need, and so forth. Second, when I say that generosity implies going beyond what is due, I am referring to what is due to the beneficiaries. It is simply justice to give what is due to them. Our responsibility to go the extra mile, however, lies in our responsibility to grow in self-transcendence beyond such minimums. Put simply, we must grow in love, even though no one can say, "You owe me love."

Another difficulty is this: Does not the responsibility to grow in virtue undermine generosity since generous people give freely and gladly, out of desire and not obligation? First, we can and should freely desire to do what we ought to do. Second, having an obligation is not the same as acting out of a sense of obligation. We have an obligation to eat, but we usually eat not out of a feeling of duty but out of a desire for pleasure and nourishment. Similarly, we act generously out of an experience of joy and love, not constraint. The experience of obligation likely is a sign that there is resistance in ourselves to doing spontaneously what we ought to do. In short, we ought to be generous, and we fail morally if we are never or rarely generous. In the act of being generous, however, we will not ordinarily experience ourselves as acting under obligation but rather as acting freely and with joy. It is not enough to do "loving deeds"; it is also necessary to have a loving heart (1 Cor 13:1-3; Acts 8:19-21).

### Originating in Love

What's love got to do with it? Our moral responsibility to become generous derives from our threefold moral responsibility to love ourselves, to love others, and to love God. Regularly to fail to act generously is both a failure in love for ourselves, that is, to develop an important human excellence, and a failure in love for others, that is, to transcend ourselves in creativity on behalf of their maintenance and growth. (More fundamentally, as we will see near the end of this essay, it is also a failure in cooperating with God's love, which is the ultimate criterion of morality.[38])

1. *Self-love:* In the present order of salvation, we humans are both sinners and saints. Because we are naturally selfish and inclined to sin, we need to be wary of self-love. Because we are created good and oriented toward perfection, however, and because we are so psychologically and physically fragile, we can and must love ourselves. That is, we must affectively participate in our own maintenance and development. Indeed, we are the ones most responsible for ourselves. Attentive to our own growth, we fail morally if we are not growing in the virtue of generosity.

Still, generosity is the sort of virtue we develop, so to speak, only out of the corner of our eye. If we act generously mainly in order to develop the virtue of generosity, we are not generous.[39] Our spirit remains turned in on itself and is not expansively directed to the recipients. Those who try to save their lives in this regard will lose them. Hence, the connection between generosity and self-love ordinarily will arise not as a sense that we owe it to ourselves to be generous, but as a sense that we have failed to grow toward our best selves when we have not acted generously.

2. *Other-love:* As self-transcending beings, we care not only for our own growth but also for others' growth. Through love, we emotionally participate in the lives of others in a manner that affirms their good, not only their present good but also their ideal good. Love inspires us occasionally to be "excessive." We delight in helping those we love to at least partially and momentarily partake of perfection. Love makes it easy for us to go out of our way to promote the ideal good of those we love.

Generosity to others is not confined to Christianity. Pagan philosophers long ago saw that we are by nature generous. Cicero wrote, "There is something in our nature that impels us to the open hand and heart."[40] Aristotle once asked rhetorically why we would want to have possessions if not to share them with friends.[41] Most of us like to benefit people, and the pleasure we take in doing a generous act indicates that acting generously fulfills human nature.

### God's Generosity

Is generosity also a divine trait? Considering the seven aspects of generosity which I will now discuss, it seems that God's generosity is clear in some respects and not in others.

1. *Greatly Beneficial:* We saw that "generous" applies not only to the giver but also to the gift in relation to the need of the recipient. If we focus on the latter, then surely God's gifts are superabundantly generous. We need existence, and God creates us. We need sustenance, and God provides a world of material, cultural, and social goods for us. We need redemption, and God offers forgiveness and friendship. We absolutely need these "unearned benefits," and God offers them.

2. *Intentional:* If, however, we focus on the giver and the receivers, the question of God's generosity becomes more complicated. Of course, fundamental matters are clear to most Christians: God loves us, and so, regarding the "intention to benefit," God is straightforwardly generous. Still there remain at least two questions.

The first asks whether God primarily intends our good or God's good. We saw above that someone who gives only or primarily to get is not generous. There are strands of the tradition that, in focusing on the sovereignty of God, seem to say that God acts primarily for God's sake. For example, the Bible indicates that God gives gifts in order to express God's goodness and to gain glory (Ex 14:4, 17–18; Is 43:7, 48:9–13; Jer 13:11; Jn 9:3, 11:4). Yahweh announces: "It is not for your sake, O house of Israel, that I am about to act, but for the sake of my holy name" (Ez 36:22). Accordingly, God creates and destines human beings to "live for the praise of his glory" (Eph 1:5–6, 12). Similarly, according to the First Vatican Council, the reason God creates is "to manifest His perfection"; they condemned anyone who "denies that the world was made for the glory of God."[42] If this were all that could be said, then it would seem that God is good to us, but not generous. Still, Christian tradition has long experienced God's love as *agape:* Beyond anything we deserve, God creates and redeems us for our own sakes, not simply for God's sake.[43] "God proves his love for us in that while we were still sinners Christ died for us" (Rm 5:8).

The second and harder question asks whether God intends to benefit each of us or perhaps only some of us or maybe only humanity as a whole or even only creation as a whole.[44] While Israel remembered God's killing of innocent Egyptians as a special favor done for them (Ex 12:12), the Egyptians (and others since) must have been hard pressed to see God as generous to them. Similarly, in John's Gospel, Jesus says that God loves the "world"; but then Jesus explains that this love leads to the salvation of believers, while nonbelievers are already condemned (Jn 3:16–18). In Luke, Jesus suggests that God guards the narrow door leading to salvation and refuses to even acknowledge some who beg for entrance (Lk 13:23–25). Moreover, certain prominent strands of the subsequent tradition have been confident that God predestines some people for hell. Even Aquinas argued that although God wills diverse goods for every human being, God does not will the good of eternal life for everyone.[45] Should we say that God is generous to people if they will spend eternity in hell?

Similarly, it is not crystal clear whether God directly benefits even the saved in each good that comes to them or only in the whole of their lives or, again, only in the afterlife. In Margaret Farley's stark and challenging words: "God does not always do the deeds that are expected, even when they are desperately needed.... God appears not only as one who does not fulfill what is promised but as one who abandons, uses, excludes, conspires against, defeats, hands over to be raped and killed."[46] Although generous donors ought not take back their gifts, the Lord who gives also takes away (Jb 1:21; Dt 6:10–15; Pss 52:7, 104:29; cf. Rm 11:29). A desire to distance God from evil and a recognition that good people sometimes lose out has led some theologians to assert only a more general or holistic benevolence.[47]

Otherwise, they hold, when a car swerves to miss my child playing in the street but thereby kills your child, if we say that God intended to benefit my child, how can we avoid saying that God intended to kill your child?

The tradition has in the main wanted to say that God gives all individuals each and every good that comes to them. Accordingly, it has been necessary to admit that God distributes gifts quite unequally. For example, God is partial to Israel: "Yet the LORD set his heart in love on your ancestors alone and chose you, their descendants after them, out of all peoples" (Dt 10:15; also Ps 147:20). For special favors God singles out David (1 Sm 16:6–13), Mary (Lk 1:28), Jesus (Jn 1:14), the twelve (Lk 6:12–16), Paul (Gal 1:12–16), and particular communities (1 Cor 1:1–12). And within the body of Christ, God gives greater and lesser gifts to different members (1 Cor 12:4–11; Rm 12:3). Thomas Aquinas concluded from the unequal distribution of goods that God does not love all people equally and thus is not equally generous to all.[48] I will return to this question of the distribution of God's gifts—including the problem of evil—when I take up the topic of gratitude.

From the conflicting material of this section, perhaps all we can say is that there has been considerable diversity in church tradition about the range of God's generosity. Some say the sovereign God is generous to whomever and in whatever way God chooses. Others, including myself, say that God's generosity primarily refers to God's proper activities, such as creation and redemption, and only secondarily and derivatively to any intraworldly goods. The basic act of God's love is to will the salvation of all (cf. 1 Tm 2:4).

3. *Conditional:* The biblical God clearly offers conditioned gifts. God decides who will benefit from the gift, how it should be used, or how the recipient should respond. Are these conditions compatible with generosity?

The theocentric strand of scripture, which shares elements of the "big man" pattern of giving, often pictures God as giving gifts in view of some benefit to God. Ordinarily, generous donors should not demand a response or a return gift,[49] but the biblical God demands gifts and sets down precisely how we are to respond (Dt 12:11–28, 26:1–11). For example, in response to divine blessings, Yahweh often demanded obedient service (1 Sm 15:22).[50] If people obeyed, God promised further gifts; but if they disobeyed, they received the worst of evils (Dt 28:1–2, 15, 30:15–20). Yahweh insisted that no one should approach God empty-handed (Ex 23:15). Nevertheless, God did not welcome the sacrifices that people chose to offer, no matter how excellent the gifts. Rather, Yahweh prescribed certain festivals, specified return gifts, and gave precise instructions for how various gifts were to be offered (Ex 30:12, 34:20; Dt 12:13–28, 14:22–27, 16:16). All these conditions are appropriate in a theocentric context of God's sovereignty. But they also diminish the spirit of liberality that ordinarily characterizes generosity.

There are, however, other conditions that, perhaps, are open to an alternate anthropocentric interpretation. These conditions intrinsically promote human life, especially communal life. If so, God's *agape* is more evident in these conditions. For example, those who are forgiven but do not forgive will have their debt restored; those who are given other gifts but are not generous to others will lose their present gifts and not receive any future gifts (Mt 18:23–35, 25:46; Lk 6:37–38, 14:12–14, 19:15–26; Phil 4:7). It would be easy to argue that these kinds of conditions also make the same theocentric point—namely, "Use these gifts as I say, or I will take them back." Perhaps we may, however, without too much stretching, interpret them to underscore an anthropological truth: Those who refuse to forgive after being forgiven are deficient as human beings, and thus they

will decline in their humanity; those who do not act generously or work productively for others are people whose lives
lack something important, and thus they will deteriorate as
human beings.

These kinds of conditions also suggest a more explicitly
theanthropocentric interpretation: God wants to forgive and
help others, and those who do not forgive and help others
are not cooperating with God and to that degree are not in
union with God. In that sense, those who are not generous
will lose (the very religious point of) the gifts they already
have. In short, if we may interpret the conditions that God
places on gifts as motivated by agape and philia, then many
of these conditions intrinsically promote human and
Christian life, and thus they spring from God's generosity.

4. *Costly:* Gifts usually represent some effort or cost to
the donor, but, unlike the widow's mite (Mk 12:41–44), gift-
giving seems to cost God nothing. The sovereign God speaks,
and the deed is done. This God cannot be "hurt" by our failure to respond or to properly use divine gifts. Thus, this God
gives and does not count the costs, because for this God there
can be no costs. If that is the case, is God generous?

I have two responses: First, the criterion of "costliness"
really is only an indicator for the self-gift of love. This criterion rightly insists that what is given should be valuable to
the giver. It is a common mistake, however, to think that all
love is self-sacrificial. Rather, gifts of love often are given
with joy and a sense of fulfillment. Thus God's gifts may not
"cost" God anything, yet they may still be valuable to God as
expressions or enactments of God's overflowing love for us.

Second, to many Christians, it is not at all clear that
there are no costs for God in creating and redeeming us.
When John writes that "God so loved the world that he gave
his only Son" (Jn 3:16), these Christians find it impossible to
think that the passion of Christ was not costly for his Abba.

For these theologians, among whom I count myself, a God who truly loves us is vulnerable to disappointment and frustration whenever we perversely or defiantly use God's gifts (Jer 2:5, 20). The God who has entered into a mutual love relationship with us knows the cost involved in sharing life with people who are so needy and sinful. Paul exhorts us to bear one another's burdens (Gal 6:2); and, in Christ, God also chooses generously to bear our sufferings, failures, finitude, and even our sin (Phil 2:6; Heb 4:15, 5:8, 9:28).[51]

5. *Obligation:* Lastly, does God have any obligation to be generous to us? The very idea that God has obligations may seem preposterous. The usual theological answer would be that God is sovereignly free and thus has no obligations to us or anyone else. Still, we may reconsider this theological claim. If God is more fundamentally "love partner" than sovereign Lord, then God may also have the obligations that attend God's self-love, God's agapic love for us, and God's covenant with us.

First, we can presume that God loves God's self. If God has generously decided to be creator, redeemer, and sanctifier, then presumably out of fidelity to God's own self God has a responsibility to be engaged in these generous activities. Second, God has responsibilities that flow from God's fidelity to our selves. We would rightly fault parents who gave birth and then abandoned their children. Accordingly, we can presume that God, like our parents and other creators, has something of a personal obligation to support us (cf. Is 49:15). Jesus himself used a "how much more" argument to go from human parents to our "Father in heaven" (Mt 7:10). In other words, God does not owe us existence; but once God creates us, God has responsibilities toward us.

To say that God has obligations is not to negate God's generosity. Out of generosity, God creates and redeems us. God's subsequent care partakes of that original generosity.

Thus, God's participation in our lives is, on our part, experienced as an overwhelming act of continuing, undeserved generosity. In short, love ordinarily entails great responsibilities; nonetheless love is received as the most generous gift.

## GRATITUDE

Authors as diverse as Ignatius of Loyola, Immanuel Kant, Thomas Aquinas, and William Shakespeare have written that ingratitude is among the worst of sins.[52] One Hindu scripture claims: "Those who slaughter cows, drink wine and break promises can be saved; but there is no salvation for an ungrateful person."[53] Most of us would not agree with these assessments. Indeed, many people with whom I have spoken adamantly deny any moral obligation to be grateful. Some biblical scholars claim that expressions of gratitude not only are not "natural" but also are not even present in many cultures, including those of biblical Israel.[54] I will try to show that we ought to be grateful to our benefactors. First, however, I want to address three obstacles to gratitude.

### Obstacles to Gratitude

The first two obstacles are located in pathologies of the self: on the one hand, individualism that overvalues the independent self and, on the other hand, a lack of self-love which undervalues that self. According to an individualist, we are not dependent on others, and we alone should determine what we are to do. Strong individualists imagine themselves to be self-made persons who have earned whatever they have. They accept no obligations except those they freely choose. This kind of individualism has no place for gratitude which implies that who we are, what we do, and what we have is dependent upon the contributions of others. It also implies that we have obligations, for example, to our parents, that we did not choose.

Gratitude is similarly difficult where there is little sense of self. That may occur in cultures that are highly communal and highly structured.[55] Even in our individualist culture, however, there are many who lack a lively self-love. When we do not love ourselves, we can observe the gift given; we can receive it; and we may even make an intellectual judgment that the gift is good for ourselves. Nonetheless, without self-love we cannot be grateful, because gratitude includes emotionally affirming and being glad about our self that has benefited. Indeed, the deeper the self-love, the deeper the possibility of gratitude. We Christians are sometimes exhorted to forget ourselves and be selfless, but we cannot do this and be grateful.

For socially sensitive people, the third obstacle to gratitude is the array of evils and comparative disadvantages that confront us all.[56] If life is a bowl of cherries, some of those cherries are sour, others are rotten, and a few even poisonously fatal; moreover, if there are good cherries in our bowl, those cherries cannot be in the bowls of others who may be more hungry. Some Christians exhort one another to give thanks even for evil.[57] Those of us with a sensitive conscience, however, will have difficulties giving thanks "always and everywhere" (Eph 5:20; 1 Tm 4:4), since most of our blessings either involve deprivations for others or give us a comparative advantage over them. Much in life approximates a competitive zero-sum game. Should I give thanks if I find the last parking spot, since my good fortune means someone else goes without it? Should we be grateful for our parishioners' generous gifts to the church building fund, if that likely means they will not contribute to the neighborhood homeless shelter? Should my daughter give thanks for her quick insight if that means that others with less self-esteem will be passed over for not being as smart?

*Characteristics of Gratitude*

Like generosity, gratitude is a relative term. We are more or less grateful depending on the gift, our need, and the generosity of the donor. Gratitude has three constituent phases: reception of the gift, response to the giver, and grateful use of the gift. These phases need not occur in order. For example, as children we happily used the gifts our parents gave us long before we were able to express our thanks. Indeed, even as adults we often skip from reception to use, with nary a nod of response.

1. *Reception:* Gratitude essentially involves a phase in which we gladly welcome the contribution another makes to our lives. Gratitude is an affective virtue.[58] To use Aquinas's words, "Gratitude depends chiefly on the heart."[59] We are moved not only by the gift itself and how it enriches our lives, but also by the donor's goodness. These feelings cannot be directly willed, but their spontaneous stirring can be fostered.[60] Such receptivity is essential to a moral life. Often it takes a well-balanced person, who has considerably overcome narcissism, to be able to receive without distortion what other people offer. Moreover, in a mature philia-love, persons open themselves to being acted upon as well as to act.[61] The welcoming phase of gratitude highlights this important dimension of human life.

Gratitude essentially has a "for me" or "for mine" quality.[62] We can, properly speaking, give thanks only when we or persons whose lives we share have been benefited. We can be happy that a stranger has won the lottery, but not thankful. Thus, some spiritual writers offer inconsistent advice when they simultaneously claim that we should be grateful for all God gives us and that what God gives us is not for us but is to be passed on to others. Rather, we can be grateful only if, in some sense, the gift is meant for our betterment. Of course, we might feel grateful to be chosen to be God's agent in this distribution, since that privilege is one of the best benefits God can bestow.

2. *Response:* The second constituent of gratitude is an affective response to the donor. If, without feeling, we respond to the donor simply "out of duty" or "social convention" or for self-interested reasons, our response may be correct, but we are not grateful.[63] In offering a grateful response, we get beyond a childish tendency to treat others as extensions of ourselves or as servants of our needs.

Gratitude is a response not merely to benefits, but also to someone's benevolence.[64] Since the various goods we receive bear a reference to the goodness of our donors, we turn favorably to them.[65] When they have incurred some loss in benefiting us, we respond not so much with compassion or regret at their loss as with a positive affirmation of their generosity. Underlying our response is the natural inclination to respond to love with love. There may, of course, be good reasons why, in particular cases, we cannot or should not respond to the donor. But non-response is an absence of what ideally should happen. This mixture of fullness (i.e., a sense of expansion at being enriched that makes us want to overflow and share with others) and incompleteness (i.e., a sense of dependence and a desire to participate more in the life of the one who enriches us) stimulates in us the virtuous desire to offer a grateful response.

Often a simple "Thank you" is enough response, at least for the moment. In many cases we need not give something more in return. Generous donors want us to gain a benefit, not to bear a new burden.[66] In other cases, however, a simple gesture is not enough, particularly when the gift comes as part of a mutual relationship. Giving and receiving gifts are constitutive of such relationships. In responding to a gift from our partners, we affectively consent to our involvement with them.[67] We implicitly pledge ourselves ready, whenever possible and appropriate, to support them. We want, in due time, to give gifts to them in order to do our part in our relationship with them. Indeed, we want, where possible, to give back more than we have received.[68] That "excess" springs from love.

Usually there will be some appropriate delay before we make a return gift. Gifts promise a future for the relationship. Too quick a reply would suggest that gratitude was only a burden we were trying to cross off our list. Nevertheless, it is not the case, as some argue, that there must always be a delay.[69] Often, as in an exchange between friends at Christmas, gifts are simultaneously exchanged, and this shared experience itself enhances both the relationship and its members.

Gratitude does not require parity in a return gift.[70] In fact, the perfectly equal return would be the very gift given, but this return would be most imperfect. The return of the same gift would mean the rejection of the giver since donors offer something of themselves with their gifts. Rather, an appropriate return gift will ordinarily be different in value because it expresses a different giver, a different receiver, and a now enhanced relationship. If all we can do is gratefully receive a gift and in return offer our thanks, that is enough.[71] When we can do more, however, we would be at fault not to do so. Our response should be guided by a consideration of the original gift, our own resources, the needs of the donor, the type of relationship we share, and various other circumstances.[72] For example, we send a birthday card to a friend who calls us on our birthday; but we open our homes to our aging parents who for many years spent themselves on our behalf.

3. *Grateful Use:* Gratitude includes not only reception and response but also grateful use of the gift. That is, gratitude includes using well the gifts we have received.[73] Were

we to misuse or abuse the gift, we would be showing disregard or even contempt for the donor, not gratitude. Still, contrary to what some write, we need not treasure all the gifts we receive, even those from God. Some gifts are to be consumed or destroyed, others are tools for our endeavors, and still others are to be developed. Each gift should be used appropriately. If someone gives us life, we should live that life well. If someone shares their knowledge with us, we likely should not only use it but also share that knowledge with others. If someone gives us herself in love, we should reverence her gift as well as foster her growth.

A gift is not ours to use as we will. When an aunt gives us money for books, we do not properly use the gift to buy a soccer ball. We do not even use it properly if we donate the money to the poor. When judge John Noonan wrote, "The gift once given is wholly the donee's and no one else's,"[74] he may have been right in law, but he is wrong in matters of gratitude. Rather, the gift continues to belong to both donor and donee, though in very different ways. As a consequence, gratitude requires us to respect any conditions placed by the donor on the gift.

## Moral Responsibility to Be Grateful

Must we be grateful? As we have seen, several great historical figures thought that gratitude was an extremely strong religious and moral obligation. Many people today, however, think of it as a pleasantry, an optional matter of etiquette. Some of my theology students react quite negatively to the proposal that gratitude is even a moral issue.[75]

Gratitude is, to be sure, a peculiar moral obligation.[76] Donors ordinarily should not demand a response;[77] otherwise, it is likely that they have not given a "gift" but rather made a loan or entered into a contract. When a donor says "Don't mention it" or "It was nothing," she is signaling that this gift is not part of an economic exchange. Nevertheless, in receiving a gift, we often accept various and sometimes long-term responsibilities. That is why at times we should refuse gifts.

Among the responsibilities usually is a "duty" to make some sort of response.[78] As Jane English observes, a man who has taken a woman out on a date cannot demand a favor in return. On the other hand, assuming that it was a pleasant evening, it would be a defect in her character if she did not feel gratitude and want to show it in some way.[79] If this is so, however, as some object, the obligation to offer a return shows that the woman's response is merely part of an implicit contract she made in going out on a date: "Show me a nice time, and then I'll show you my gratitude." Further, they argue, her subsequent obligation nullifies his original generosity. He could not have given a gift because, since she is obligated to make a return, he too was just entering into an implied contract.[80] The debt of gratitude, on this account, turns out to be a matter of commutative justice—in principle not much different from paying someone for painting the house.[81]

A "debt of gratitude" is real, but we misunderstand gratitude if we think of it as "repaying a debt" or "restoring an imbalance."[82] In contractual justice, paying a debt discharges it and terminates the relationship. But in the language of Immanuel Kant, gratitude is a "sacred" duty since the "debt" of gratitude can never finally be repaid.[83] Moreover, as Claudia Card importantly notes, unlike the act that discharges a contractual obligation, an act of gratitude "tends to *affirm* the relationship rather than to bring it to a close; the ties are extended, deepened."[84] A grateful response does not terminate a relationship but rather begins a new phase in its give-and-take. Over time, this debt—the "debt" of love—should grow (Rm 13:8).[85]

Why do we owe anything at all? Since we have not asked for the gift and since the donor has freely given it to us, we would seem to have no responsibility to give thanks, but we do. Our debt of gratitude arises because we owe something of our lives to the generosity of others. Our lives have been changed for the better, and this improvement is due to their goodness.[86] When we welcome a beneficial change, we are compelled by the truth to accept our connectedness to its source. Our grateful response, then, is an honest recognition and glad affirmation of this connection. It is a defect of mind and character to refuse to acknowledge a reality that has benefited us. Still, our responsibility to assent to this truth does not sufficiently clarify our debt of gratitude.

We are naturally inclined to love those who love us. When people have opened themselves to us and shown themselves benevolent toward us, our responsive heart inclines toward affectively affirming them. In so doing, we fulfill our own nature, affectively enter their lives, and coop-erate in a small way with what God is trying to do on earth. We can, of course, resist or restrain our self-transcending drive to respond with love, and in this life there frequently are good reasons to do so, including dangers to ourselves as well as limits of time and energy. Unless there are such countervailing reasons, however, we have a moral and reli-gious responsibility to complete the circle of love. The degree of our involvement varies, of course: A slight benefit usually evokes and deserves a slight response of love. Still, in varying degrees, we fulfill our responsibility to love when gratitude moves us to affirm the goodness of donors, praise them for enriching us, and either create or strengthen a bond between ourselves and them.[87]

### Gratitude (Perhaps) Leading to Generosity

Does gratitude help us to be more generous with others? Before hastily answering "Yes," we should ask our-selves why the fortunate often are far less generous than others. We should also ask ourselves about fellow Christians who seem quite grateful to God, but are not very generous to others. The transition from grateful receiving to generous giving is far from automatic.

Indeed, contrary to what is often thought, gratitude includes several characteristics that, if stressed, lead to the opposite of generosity. As we have seen, gratitude essentially includes a phase where we consciously attend to ourselves and gladly affirm that we are blessed. The first temptation is to think of our blessings as our just desert. The second temptation is that, in attending to ourselves, we become forgetful of others. The third temptation is greediness for yet more blessings. Fourth, since joy and suffering do not easily share the same bed, when we give glad thanks for something good in our lives, we easily become blind, at least momentarily, to all the people of the world who are in misery. Fifth, we will be especially inclined to harden our hearts or narrow our vision when our good fortune has come at another's expense. Israel praised God not only for delivering it from Egypt, but also for crushing even innocent Egyptians (Ex 15:1–21). Thus, gratitude too often walks tall by forgetting others who have been laid low.

Additionally, gratitude is commonly stimulated by comparing ourselves to people who are less well off. We ordinarily do not thank God for our nice home until we see people living in a shanty. If we give thanks for our intelligence or our outgoing personality, we give thanks for gifts that, in fact, give us a largely unearned advantage over others. Such gratitude walks perilously near the Pharisee who says "God, I thank you that I am not like other people" (Lk 18:11–13). In brief, if gratitude to God is not complemented by self-transcending love of others, it can feed selfishness and is hardly a noble Christian virtue.

Nevertheless, gratitude can nourish generosity. Goodness tends to overflow. When others enrich us, we have an impulse to share the good we have received. Their generosity tends to beget our generosity.[88] If so, we freely give what we have freely received (Mt 10:8); we are merciful as God is merciful (Mt 18:32–33; Lk 6:36). By this overflowing of gratitude into generosity towards others I do not mean that God gives us gifts so that we will pass them on to others. If someone gives us something just to hand it on to others, he has not given us a gift. Rather, God gives us gifts and they are ours. After we receive these gifts, our self-transcendence itself enables and, indeed, requires us to move outward toward benefiting others. When this happens, gratitude for God's generosity to us inspires our own generosity as an overflow of a full heart.

### Gratitude to God

Should we be grateful to God? The argument for gratitude to God has seemed obvious. God offers us the gifts of our creation and salvation. Understanding ourselves to be so gifted by God, we of course should offer prayers of thanksgiving to God (Ps 107:1; Col 3:16–17; 1 Tm 4:4; 2 Cor 4:15; Heb 12:28). By our gratitude, we not only acknowledge and rejoice in our dependence on God, but we also develop our mutual relationship with God. By giving us everything, God does not unfairly burden us with what Satan in Milton's *Paradise Lost* protested as "The debt immense of endless gratitude."[89] Rather, this debt, paradoxically, pays rewards forever. In short, our moral and religious responsibility to give thanks to God has seemed abundantly clear to Christians. Nevertheless, this responsibility is actually filled with troublesome issues. Let me discuss some of these in terms of gratitude's three constituent phases: reception, response, and use.

1. *Reception:* The most difficult question to answer is what we should be grateful for. The answer is not as simple as Paul's exhortation to give thanks for everything "always and everywhere" (Eph 5:20; 1 Thes 5:18; 1 Tm 4:4). Should we thank God if all the traffic lights are green on the day that we leave home late for work? What if they are all red and we get fired? Trying to give thanks for everything would blind us to genuine evils such as disease and disasters, sin and suffering. As members of a religion of salvation, we Christians must take account of these evils. Our self-transcendence does not mean the denial of reality but rather the ability to deal with it either by overcoming it or by contextualizing it within our life-journey.

Paul's exhortation presupposes, instead, a love relationship with God. Lovers commonly see everything in light of their relationship. Everything that supports or enhances the relationship is welcomed; everything that threatens it is resisted or rejected; everything else remains affectively on the margin. Similarly, when we are involved in a mutual love with God, we are confident that any good that comes our way originates from the God who loves us and shares our life. Hence, we give thanks for everything (good). But when we experience something as not truly good for us or our relationship with God, we trust that God does not want it for us and is opposed to such evil. Hence, we attribute the evil to some other source, such as sinful humanity or chaotic nature. We do not and should not thank God for such evils. This process of attributing good to God and evil to other sources is not, of course, a deductive process. Rather, it is the logic of a philia-love at work.

The greatness of religious gratitude is that it affectively connects us both to our own lives and to God as our benefactor. For these two reasons, gratitude is an enormously important Christian virtue. But its danger is that it usually lacks compelling reference to others, since gratitude is typically a "here and now" and "for me and mine" experience. Some of our best gifts are directly connected to others' losses (Is 43:3–4; Rm 5:10, 15). Should we thank God that a steady rain revivifies our parched crops? What if our neighbor had planned an outdoor wedding party on that day? We need the self-transcending power of love and the critical, universalizing power of reason to keep us mindful of others who may be disadvantaged by our gain or who do not have as good a life as we do. Without this self-transcendence, religious gratitude may only be an *egoisme à deux* between God and ourselves.

Thus, gratitude has its place, but often it must rhythmically give way, say, to compassion for those who are less fortunate than ourselves and especially for those who lose because we gain. We might find ourselves with deep emotion thanking God that we got bumped from the plane that crashed in the ocean; but first we should have been filled with horror for all the passengers who died. "For everything (including such virtues) there is a season...a time to mourn, and a time to dance" (Eccl 3:1).

2. *Response:* Upon recognizing and welcoming God's gifts, we should not leap immediately to grateful use of those gifts. Action, even good action on behalf of our neighbors, is no substitute for a direct response to God. Just as love of neighbor does not replace a love for God, so the proper use of creation is not sufficient for showing gratitude to God.[90] The gifts we receive from God range from absolute to minor, from our existence and redemption to our morning cup of coffee. Different responses of gratitude accordingly are called for, from the complete dedication of our lives (Ps 116:12–13) to a momentary "Thank you, Jesus."

Surprisingly, however, the classical image of a sovereign God inclines us in three ways to omit a direct response to God. First, if it costs nothing for the absolutely sovereign God to provide benefits, we have diminished impetus to thank God for being generous. Second, since this God is said to possess all good and be the owner of everything, there seems to be nothing we can give in return to God.[91] Third, offering gratitude to God seems to be a futile gesture since the completely self-sufficient God cannot really receive our offer. A gesture of gratitude might be good for us, but it is good in the way we feel a need to wave our hand to a parting friend who has already driven around the corner. In the face of these three obstacles, some theologians have concluded that, instead of trying futilely to offer grateful response to the sovereign God, we should just willingly open our hands to receive more and get on with our life in the world.[92] Thus, one curious consequence of imagining God as beyond any response of ours is that we seem to have no alternative but to act anthropocentrically.[93] God becomes a mere "means or provider" of goods for ourselves.[94]

This theological stance, oddly enough, is not too distant from that of people who are practical or theoretical atheists. Atheists use life's goods without giving thanks to God. They can, of course, be grateful to particular persons or institutions, and they can be "cosmically" grateful.[95] For example, they are grateful that the flood damage was not worse, or they are grateful that they sold their stocks before the market crashed. For atheists, the referent of this cosmic emotion of gratitude may be as diffuse as "lucky stars." Such cosmic emotion should not be discounted. It is one way that we human beings acknowledge we are not self-sufficient and, more importantly, that we point to a larger, metaphysical realm. For atheists, however, no more can be said. They can celebrate life and the world, but they cannot worship.[96]

Why should Christians thank God, however, when it is the eye surgeon who skillfully restores our sight? God does not (at least ordinarily) intervene to steady the physician's hand or keep the laser working, but still it is God who gives these creatures their existence, power, and direction.[97] The eye surgeon, knowingly or unknowingly, cooperates with God. Without God, she would literally be nothing, and so we are grateful not only to her but to God as well.

The authors cited at the beginning of this essay rightly argue that we must give thanks to God. Still, they mislead us with their contention that gratitude is the core of the Christian life. Rather, love is the core virtue. Expressions of explicit gratitude may express that core, but they may also be a sign of distance. Indeed, gratitude often betokens reserve and separation. I have spoken with Christians who give thanks to God throughout their day. For them, however, frequent expression of gratitude does not constitute intimacy with God. The God they thank seems like a philanthropist living in a far-off land. Their experience shows that intimacy with God is a separate gift that no amount of giving thanks can produce.

When a beloved gives us her own heart, the appropriate response is not to say "Thank you" but to love in return. When two friends have spent a wonderful day together, if they say "thank you" at all, it likely will only be as they separate. Rather, friends tend to express their love by telling stories about the good times they have had together. Perhaps that is why biblical authors tended not to say thank you to God but rather to recount all the ways that God had blessed them.[98]

Still, if we are gifted with intimacy with God, then as lovers we will feel exceedingly grateful for the love we share. The most profound gratitude to God takes place within an on-going friendship with God. God is involved with us, caring for us in a compassionate, even motherly way (Ex 3:7; Ps 103; Is 49:15–16, 66:13; Hos 11:8–9; Jer 8:18). For this, our soul gives thanks. Our principal response to God's love, however, is not expressions of thanks; rather, it is to love

God in return and, through that union, also to love those whom God loves (Dt 4:37, 6:5; Mt 22:37–40).

3. *Grateful Use:* The third constituent of gratitude consists in using well what we have been given. Otherwise, God will have given in vain. *Use,* of course, is a loose term. For example, we "use" the gift of our lives by nourishing our bodies and developing our talents. We "gratefully use" the gift of friends by cherishing them.

Grateful use requires us to use the gifts in accord with the conditions the donor sets down. Sometimes these conditions are intrinsic. That is, they flow from the very nature of the gift. Other times they are extrinsic. In the biblical tradition, God's gifts frequently seem to be accompanied by extrinsic conditions. Yahweh enjoined Israel to obey an immense array of commandments, laws, and customs as conditions of God's favor (Dt 11:32).[99] Israel obeyed these conditions with the awareness that compliance would be followed by long life and abundant blessings. Noncompliance promised curses and death (Dt 11:1–9, 30:15–16; Ps 103:7–21; Jer 9:10–12).[100] In the postbiblical period, the church has moved toward understanding the conditions set on God's gifts as intrinsic. For example, John Paul II wrote, "In giving life to man, God demands that he love, respect and promote life. The gift thus becomes a commandment."[101] The very nature of human life commands our respect and love. While extrinsic conditions easily fit within a divine command ethic, intrinsic conditions provide a theological foundation for a natural law ethic. In our friendship with God, God places fewer extrinsic conditions on God's gifts, and God offers greater latitude even in respect to intrinsic conditions. Partners in a *philia*-love relationship accord one another considerable leeway in the use of gifts in order to enhance the freedom and trust that are essential in such a relationship.

*Return Gifts for God*

We saw above that in many situations a "Thank you" suffices as a response. When the gift expresses and contributes to a mutual relationship, however, a return gift is frequently necessary, otherwise the relationship likely will cease being mutual. Nonetheless, we seem unable to give God anything (Rm 11:35–36). Although an early biblical tradition thought that we should provide nourishment and pleasure to God (Lv 21:6; Nm 28:2, 27), the psalmist subsequently made it clear that God has, after all, no need for cereal and blood offerings (Ps 40:6–8, 50:12–14, 51:16–17). Rather, God wants our hearts. That is something we can offer that God does not already have. When Christ the high priest offers a fragrant, sacrificial offering to God, what he offers is "himself" (Eph 5:2; Heb 5:1, 8:3–4, 9:12–14). We too can offer spiritual gifts, namely, our own selves (Rm 12:1; 1 Pt 2:5, 9).

An analogy may help. Even in human relationships, we can give gifts to the "man who has everything." Although we may not be able to give rich persons some item they do not already have or could not obtain, we can still give them something they do not have, namely, a "gift from us." Another analogy: Children get money from their parents so that they can then give gifts to their parents. The fishing rod a daughter therewith buys for her dad is more valuable than a similar rod he buys for himself. The basic idea is that our benefactors do not have our love unless we freely give it to them.

Analogously, even though God may be infinitely "rich" and the source of all good, we can give God at least three types of gifts that God does not have. First and most importantly, we can and should offer ourselves to God. That is, we can love God. When Christ offered himself to God, we assume that this was a real gift to God and a gift that God received (Heb 9:24, 10:12). Similarly, we too can give ourselves. This is a gift that God otherwise does not have. Classical theology often argued that God needs nothing and can receive nothing. By contrast, the Bible and many prayerful people envision God as the one maximally able both to receive and to be moved by the prayers and needs of many. In the latter view, God is receptive to our gift of love.[102]

Second, we can reserve certain creatures to God, setting them apart from profane use. In an ancient sense of the word, these creatures then become "holy." For example, the "pointless waste" of sacrificing a heifer indicated that Israelites lived for God and not just for earthly concerns (Nm 19:2–10). Similarly, our restrictive designation of certain buildings as churches reserves them for religious purposes. Nevertheless, some might ask, how can we reserve some creatures for God when all creatures already belong to God (Dt 10:14; Ex 19:5; 1 Chr 29:11–12; 1 Cor 10:26)? This objection is mistaken: When God gives us the goods of creation, they become genuinely "ours." Thus they are ours to give back to God. Just as within a family, individuals have ownership yet all is owned by the family, so also we have ownership even though all belongs to God in our mutual relationship.

Third, in response to God's generosity, we can and should be generous to others, and we should do so freely, eagerly, and cheerfully (Jb 35:8; 2 Cor 8:9–14, 9:5–7).[103] Our good acts toward others are offerings that please the God who has gifted us (Mt 10:8; Phil 4:18; Eph 4:32; Heb 13:16; 1 Pt 4:10). Still, we must ask why helping *others* is a way of expressing gratitude to *God.* Ordinarily, being generous to one person does not count as being grateful to another. Three answers may be suggested here. First, we sometimes help the child of our friends as a way of helping them. Such action is genuinely beneficial to them since their child is really related to them.[104] Thus, we can offer return gifts to God by being good to the children of God, to those with whom Christ identifies (Mt 25:31–40; Gal 4:7). Second, if one condition placed by God on

God's gifts to us is that we benefit others, then helping others can be a form of grateful use, and thus a form of gratitude to God. We give God the pleasure of seeing God's gift bear the fruit God desires. Third, we make a return gift to others by helping them with their projects. Since God is still at work in creating, preserving, renewing, redeeming, judging, and the like, we can give a return gift to God by cooperating, to the degree we are able, in these activities of God (Jn 9:4; 1 Cor 3:9; 2 Cor 1:3–5, 2:14). In so cooperating, we help God achieve what God cannot do without us, namely, all those things that depend on our free involvement for their meaning. As a prime example, the love that God wants to show our friends through us is not replaceable by the love of anyone else. Our love for them cooperates with God and thus can be our gift to God.

In conclusion, the notions of gifts, generosity, and gratitude are complicated, and they become more so when referring to God. These three point to the essentially relational and receptive quality of human life, and they suggest revisions in the classical image of God and in classical spirituality. God and we are involved in a mutual love relationship. The giftedness of our life flows from the promise of this relationship, draws us further into its fuller realization, and drives us outward in generosity toward all that God loves.

## NOTES

1. I am grateful to the faculty of Weston Jesuit School of Theology and to the members of the Moral Theology and Spirituality conference at the Pontifical College Josephinum. They criticized two earlier versions of this essay and stimulated many useful revisions. I further want to thank Dan Harrington, John Kselman, Meg Causey, Maureen Donohue, and Helen Akinc for their special contributions.

2. James Gustafson, *Ethics from a Theocentric Perspective*, vol. 1 (Chicago: University of Chicago Press, 1981), 131; see also

Brian Gerrish, *Grace and Gratitude: Eucharistic Theology of John Calvin* (Edinburgh: T. & T. Clark, 1993), 20, 41.

3. John Koenig, "The Heartbeat of Praise and Thanksgiving," *Weavings* 7 (November/December 1992): 15.

4. Brian Childs, "Gratitude," *Dictionary of Pastoral Care and Counseling*, ed. Rodney Hunter (Nashville: Abingdon, 1990), 470-71.

5. Richard Gula, S.S., *Reason Informed by Faith* (Mahwah, N.J.: Paulist Press, 1989), 52; see Enda McDonagh, *Gift and Call* (Dublin: Gill and Macmillan, 1975), 86.

6. Paul Camenisch, "Gift and Gratitude in Ethics," *Journal of Religious Ethics* 9 (Spring 1981): 25-28.

7. Edward C. Vacek, S.J., *Anthropological Foundations of Scheler's Ethics of Love* (Ann Arbor, Mich.: University Microfilms, 1978); *Love, Human and Divine: The Heart of Christian Ethics* (Georgetown University Press, 1994); "Scheler's Phenomenology of Love," *The Journal of Religion* 62:2 (April 1982): 156-77; "Personal Growth and the '*Ordo Amoris*'," *Listening* 21:3 (Fall 1986): 197-209; "Toward a Phenomenology of Love Lost," *Journal of Phenomenological Psychology* 20:1 (Spring 1989): 1-19; "Charity," and "Love," *New Dictionary of Social Ethics*, ed. Judith Dwyer (Collegeville, Minn.: Liturgical Press, 1994), 143, 556-58; "Love, Christian and Diverse: A Response to Colin Grant," *Journal of Religious Ethics* 24:1 (Spring 1996): 29-34; "Love for God—Is It Obligatory?" *The Annual of the Society of Christian Ethics* (1996) 221-47; "Divine-Command, Natural-Law, and Mutual-Love Ethics," *Theological Studies* 57:4 (December 1996): 633-53; "The Eclipse of Love for God," *America* 174:8 (March 9, 1996): 13-16; "Religious Life and the Eclipse of Love for God," *Review for Religious* 57:2 (March-April 1998): 118-37.

8. Vacek, *Love, Human and Divine*, 157-58.

9. Vacek, *Love, Human and Divine*, 157-91; Gene Outka, *Agape* (New Haven: Yale University Press, 1976), 34.

10. William E. May, "Images that Shape the Public Obligations of the Minister," *Clergy Ethics in a Changing Society*, eds. James Wind et al. (Louisville: Westminster/John Knox Press, 1991), 65.

11. Vacek, *Love, Human and Divine*, 239-73.

12. Vacek, *Love, Human and Divine*, 280–312.

13. Claudia Card, "Gender and Moral Luck," *Identity, Character, and Morality*, eds. Owen Flanagan and Amélie Oksenberg Rorty (Cambridge, Mass.: Massachusetts Institute of Technology Press, 1990), 213–14.

14. Thomas Aquinas, *Summa Theologica* [hereafter *ST*], trans. Fathers of English Dominican Province, 5 vols. (Westminster, Md.: Christian Classics, 1981), II-II q.23 a.1.

15. Vacek, *Love, Human and Divine*, 308–12.

16. Aquinas, *ST* I q.38 a.2.

17. John Milbank, "Can a Gift Be Given?" *Modern Theology* 11 (January 1995): 127–28, 133; Thomas Murray, "Gifts of the Body and the Needs of Strangers," *Hastings Center Report* 17:2 (April 1987): 34; Jeffrey Fadiman, "Business Traveler's Guide to Gifts and Bribes," in William Shaw and Vincent Barry, *Moral Issues in Business*, 6th ed. (Belmont, Cal.: Wadsworth, 1995), 403–7; Robert Solomon, *Passion for Justice* (Lanham, Md.: Rowman & Littlefield, 1995), 89–90; Webb, *Gifting God*, 32–43, 50.

18. Milbank, "Can a Gift Be Given?" 129.

19. Camenisch, "Gift and Gratitude in Ethics," 2; Murray, "Gifts of the Body," 30–38.

20. Kenneth Schmitz, *The Gift: Creation* (Milwaukee: Marquette University Press, 1982), 45–47.

21. Richard Titmus, *Gift Relationship* (New York: Pantheon, 1971), 74; Schmitz, *Gift*, 47–48; Terrance McConnell, *Gratitude* (Philadelphia: Temple University Press, 1993), 52.

22. Lawrence Becker, *Reciprocity* (New York: Routledge & Kegan Paul, 1986), 125–26. Fred Berger, "Gratitude," *Ethics* 85 (July 1975): 299, stresses benevolence, and hence for him we cannot be grateful for acts that are not intended to help us.

23. For some basic types of gifts, see my essay, "God's Gifts and our Moral Lives," in *Method and Catholic Moral Theology: The Ongoing Reconstruction*, ed. Todd Salzman (Omaha: Creighton University Press, 1999).

24. Paul Rigby and Paul O'Grady, "Agape and Altruism," *Journal of the American Academy of Religion* 57 (1989): 721.

25. Webb, *Gifting God*, 15.

26. Webb, *Gifting God*, 20–22.

27. Webb, *Gifting God*, 4.

28. Childs, "Gratitude," 470–71; Camenisch, "Gift and Gratitude in Ethics," 3–4, 6, 8, 29; Becker, *Reciprocity*, 135.

29. Seneca, "De Beneficiis," VI, #12, *Moral Essays* (Cambridge, Mass.: Harvard University Press, 1958), 386–87.

30. Seneca, "De Beneficiis," VI, #13, 388–89.

31. Camenisch, "Gift and Gratitude in Ethics," 13, 31.

32. James Wallace, "Generosity," *Vice and Virtue in Everyday Life*, eds. Christina Sommers and Fred Sommers (New York: Harcourt Brace Jovanovich, 1993), 290.

33. Martha Nussbaum, *Fragility of Goodness* (New York: Cambridge University Press, 1987), 308–9.

34. Wallace, "Generosity," 290.

35. Edward Vacek, S.J., *Ethical Ideas in Teilhard de Chardin* (M.A. thesis, St. Louis University, 1968).

36. Karl Rahner, S.J., "The 'Commandment' of Love in Relation to the Other Commandments," *Theological Investigations* 5 (Baltimore: Helicon, 1966): 451–52.

37. Vacek, *Love, Human and Divine*, 63–66.

38. Vacek, "Divine-Command, Natural-Law, and Mutual-Love Ethics," 633–53.

39. David Sanderlin, "Charity According to St. John of the Cross," *Journal of Religious Ethics* 21 (Spring 1993): 87–115; Outka, *Agape*, 34.

40. Cicero, "On Friendship," #31, in *Other Selves*, ed. Michael Pakaluk (Indianapolis: Hackett, 1991), 91.

41. Aristotle, *Nicomachean Ethics*, 1155a, in *Basic Works of Aristotle*, ed. Richard McKeon (New York: Random House, 1941), 1058.

42. Henricus Denzinger and Adolfus Schönmetzer, S.J., eds. *Enchiridion Symbolorum*, 35th ed. (Rome: Herder, 1973), #3002, 3025; Schmitz, *Gift*, 20–24.

43. Anders Nygren, *Agape and Eros* (New York: Harper & Row, 1969).

44. Cf. Aquinas, *ST* I q.22 a.2.

45. Cf. Aquinas, *ST* I q.32 a.3.

46. Margaret Farley, *Personal Commitments* (New York: Harper & Row, 1986), 116, 120–21.

47. Roger Haight, S.J., "Foundational Issues in Jesuit Spirituality," *Studies in the Spirituality of Jesuits* 19 (September 1987): 33–35.

48. Aquinas, *ST* I q.20 a.3–4; D.A. Carson, *Divine Sovereignty and Human Responsibility* (Atlanta: John Knox Press, 1981), 197.

49. Camenisch, "Gift and Gratitude," 11; McConnell, *Gratitude,* 5.

50. William Spohn, S.J., *What Are They Saying About Scripture and Ethics?* (Mahwah, N.J.: Paulist Press, 1984), 6.

51. Lucien Richard, O.M.I., *What Are They Saying About the Theology of Suffering?* (Mahwah, N.J.: Paulist Press, 1992), 16.

52. Hugo Rahner, S.J., *Saint Ignatius Loyola: Letters to Women* (London: Nelson, 1960), 171; Immanuel Kant, *Metaphysics of Morals* (New York: Cambridge University Press, 1991), 252; Aquinas, *ST* I-II q.100 a.7; William Shakespeare, *Coriolanus* 2.3, and *Twelfth Night* 3.4, in *Complete Works of William Shakespeare* (New York: Gramercy, 1990).

53. Vasudha Narayanan, "Reciprocal Gratitude," *Spoken and Unspoken Thanks*, eds. John Carman and Frederick Streng (Cambridge, Mass.: Center for the Study of World Religions, Harvard University, 1989), 23.

54. Claus Westermann, *Praise and Lament in the Psalms* (Atlanta: John Knox Press, 1981), 25.

55. Westermann, *Praise and Lament,* 24–28.

56. Sam Keen, *Apology for Wonder* (New York: Harper & Row, 1973), 206–8.

57. Robert Roberts, *Spirituality and Human Emotions* (Grand Rapids, Mich.: Eerdmans, 1982), 77–82; Karl Rahner, S.J., "Love as the Key Virtue," *Sacramentum Mundi*, vol. 6 (New York: Herder and Herder, 1970), 344; Camenisch, "Gift and Gratitude in Ethics," 23.

58. McConnell, *Gratitude,* 81–113; Berger, "Gratitude," 305–6; Don Saliers, *Soul in Paraphrase* (New York: Seabury Press, 1980), 45–46.

59. Aquinas, *ST* II-II q.106 a.3.

60. Diana Fritz Cates, *Choosing to Feel: Virtue, Friendship, and Compassion for Friends* (Notre Dame, Ind.: University of Notre Dame Press, 1997), 179–88.

61. Margaret Farley, R.S.M., "Fragments for an Ethic of Commitment in Thomas Aquinas," *Journal of Religion* 58 (Supplement 1978): S146.

62. Vacek, *Love, Human and Divine,* 226–27.

63. John Whittaker, "'Agape' and Self-Love," *Love Commandments,* eds. Edmund Santurri and William Werpehowski (Washington, D.C.: Georgetown University Press, 1992), 237.

64. Berger, "Gratitude," 300–301.

65. William Luijpen, *Existential Phenomenology,* rev. ed. (Pittsburgh: Duquesne University Press, 1968), 315.

66. Berger, "Gratitude" 302–3.

67. Berger, "Gratitude," 302–3.

68. Aquinas, *ST* I-II q.106 a.6.

69. Milbank, "Can a Gift Be Given?" 125.

70. Berger, "Gratitude," 302–3; McConnell, *Gratitude,* 49–50.

71. Aquinas, *ST* II-II q.106 a.3; John Noonan, Jr., *Bribes* (New York: Macmillan, 1984), 695.

72. McConnell, *Gratitude,* 56.

73. Noonan, *Bribes,* 695.

74. Noonan, *Bribes,* 695.

75. Robert C. Roberts, "Emotions Among the Virtues of the Christian Life," *Journal of Religious Ethics* 20:1 (Spring 1992): 53.

76. Camenisch, "Gift and Gratitude in Ethics," 4–22; Berger, "Gratitude," 299–300; cf. Robert Roberts, "Emotions among the Virtues," 53.

77. Camenisch, "Gift and Gratitude in Ethics," 11; McConnell, *Gratitude,* 5.

78. Hans Jonas, "Philosophical Reflections on Experimenting with Human Subjects," *On Moral Medicine,* eds. Stephen Lammers and Allen Verhey (Grand Rapids, Mich.: Eerdmans, 1987), 622; David Little, "Law of Supererogation," *Love Commandments,* eds. Edmund Santurri and William Werpehowski (Washington, D.C.: Georgetown University Press, 1992), 171–75.

79. Jane English, "What Do Grown Children Owe Their Parents?" *Vice and Virtue in Everyday Life*, eds. Christina Sommers and Fred Sommers (New York: Harcourt Brace Jovanovich, 1993), 760–64; Berger, "Gratitude," 306–7.

80. Milbank, "Can a Gift Be Given?" 129–33; Joseph Lombardi, "Filial Gratitude and God's Right to Command," *Journal of Religious Ethics* 19 (Spring 1991): 110.

81. Milbank, "Can a Gift Be Given?" 125–27, mistakenly tends to understand all obligations as some form of contract.

82. Camenisch, "Gift and Gratitude in Ethics," 5–6, 12–13, 29.

83. Kant, *Metaphysics of Morals*, 250.

84. Card, "Gender and Moral Luck," 213–14.

85. Aquinas, *ST* II-II q.106 a.6; q.107 a.1.

86. Aquinas, *ST* II-II q.106 a.1, 3, 6; Lombardi, "Filial Gratitude" 107.

87. Vacek, *Love, Human and Divine*, 157–58.

88. Spohn, *What Are They Saying About Scripture and Ethics?* 121.

89. John Milton, *Paradise Lost* 4.52, in *John Milton*, eds. Stephen Orgel and Jonathan Goldberg (New York: Oxford, 1990), 422; also Aquinas, *ST* I-II q.100 a.7.

90. Vacek, "Religious Life and the Eclipse of Love for God," 118–37.

91. Outka, *Agape,* 8, 50; Daniel Maguire, *Moral Core of Judaism and Christianity* (Minneapolis: Fortress, 1993), 221.

92. Stanley Hauerwas, *The Peaceable Kingdom* (Notre Dame, Ind.: University of Notre Dame Press, 1983), 27.

93. Max Scheler, *Schriften aus dem Nachlass: III* (Bonn: Bouvier Verlag Herbert Grundmann, 1987), 218–19.

94. Roberts, *Spirituality and Human Emotions,* 80–81; Camenisch, "Gift and Gratitude in Ethics," 29; Berger, "Gratitude," 302–4.

95. Maguire, *Moral Core*, 44.

96. Keen, *Apology for Wonder,* 208–9.

97. Aquinas, *ST* I q.22 a.3.

98. Westermann, *Praise and Lament*, 25, claims that the expression "to thank" does not even occur in Hebrew.

99. Claus Westermann, *What Does the Old Testament Say About God?* (London: S.P.C.K., 1979), 18, 74, 93. To see that gratitude does not require obedience, see Lombardi, "Filial Gratitude," 93–118.

100. Vincent Brümmer, *Speaking of a Personal God* (New York: Cambridge University Press, 1992), 78–79.

101. John Paul II, *Evangelium Vitae* (The Gospel of Life), 54, in *Origins* 24:42 (April 6, 1995).

102. Farley, "Fragments for an Ethic," S146.

103. Gula, *Reason Informed by Faith*, 52.

104. Roberts, "Emotions Among the Virtues," 53–54.

*Pamela A. Smith, SS.C.M.*

# Integrating Insights:
# Morality and Parish

$\mathbb{A}$ll of us who have been steeped in the tradition of Vatican II will readily recall the way in which the Dogmatic Constitution on the Church defined the divine mandate that has been imparted to us as church. The church, we hear in *Lumen Gentium,* "receives the mission of proclaiming and establishing among all peoples the kingdom of Christ and of God." Further—and we must highlight this—"she is, on earth, the seed and the beginning of that kingdom."[1] The character of the kingdom has been richly described in the Preface for the feast of Christ the King, and *Lumen Gentium* echoes this: Christ's *basileia* is "the kingdom of truth and life, the kingdom of holiness and grace, the kingdom of justice, love, and peace."[2] All Christians, the council reminds us, "are called to the fullness of Christian life and to the perfection of love."[3] All of us, the council asserts, have vital roles to play in the transformation of the world and the realization of God's kingdom.

Since Vatican II, we Catholics—those of us, at least, who have been open to adult faith formation—have become

126

more mindful of our participation in the divine life and our dynamic ecclesial call as people of God, body of Christ, and temple of the Holy Spirit. I would like to offer several examples of people whom I have met over the past ten years whose lives reflect the call to goodness and holiness, which is moral-spiritual conversion.

Marlene is a nurse approaching retirement who has recently undertaken studies toward a master's degree in theology and is a participant in an extended study of the writings of St. John of the Cross at a Jesuit retreat center. She wants better to understand how, in her life of prayer and service, she has begun the "ascent of Mt. Carmel." She also wants to find an ecclesial setting in which to continue to learn and serve once she has retired. Her children are grown, and she has several grandchildren.

Bev is a full-time parish minister coordinating Christian service, a lay associate of a religious community, an organizer of retreats and days of renewal, and an active participant in a small parish-based group preparing spiritually for "Jubilee 2000." Not yet fifty years old, she worked for a time in an accounting firm, returned to college to gain an undergraduate degree in theology as she began parish ministry (at a distinct reduction in salary), and is this year completing a graduate degree in pastoral ministry. She has three children, the youngest of whom is a college senior.

Tom and Ted are twin brothers who were raised Lutheran but with little active involvement in denominational life. Tom converted to Catholicism in his early twenties. Ted was moved to join an RCIA group when he was in his forties and has been Catholic for only a few years. Tom drives a truck and repairs furnaces for a gas company. Ted works in a railroad freight yard. Both have a high school education. Ted became interested in the faith when Tom invited him to join him for a few sessions of a two-year lay ministry program in which Tom was engaged—a diocesan program in scripture, church history, leadership training, spiritual development, and ministerial formation. On a volunteer basis, the two have led Bible study groups, parish renewal programs, teen religious education, a youth group, and a variety of church-based service projects. They also coach athletic teams for children. Both have their own children, widely ranging in age, and Ted and his wife for the past few years have been providing foster care for pregnant teenagers and have helped them get established educationally and financially once the babies were born.

Cynthia has been active in Right to Life. After a number of years of teaching, raising children, and developing a lucrative business, she has dedicated herself to church service as a volunteer. She recently married a convert to the faith, and the couple are involved in RCIA and are helping strengthen their parish's marriage preparation program. She has taken a number of seminary courses in spirituality, ministry, moral theology, and evangelization as a way of undergirding her work in the church.

All of these are people who have benefited from and contributed to the church's threefold mission of *kerygma*, *koinonia*, and *diakonia*. They are people in whom can be found the four resources that the Canadian bishops have cited as essential for conscience formation and moral decision making and discernment: human balance, the presence of Christ, an awareness of the scriptural and traditional foundations for the moral life, and openness and adherence to the guidance of the magisterium.[4] All of them lead regular sacramental lives and have habits of daily personal prayer (spending an hour or more in the hospital chapel after a nursing shift.ends; praying the rosary daily; participating in weekday Eucharist; creating a kind of "sanctuary" with icons in the cab of a truck; writing scriptural reflections; reserving time for spiritual reading; listening meditatively to contemporary Christian music). What I have not mentioned is that each of these people has weathered grave moral crises—among them abandonment by a spouse, the suicide of a spouse, separation from a spouse, reconciliation of a marriage, marital infidelity, divorce, annulment, decisions about the aggressive or nonaggressive treatment of a dying parent, departure from the practice of the faith by a child or children, a serious threat on one's life by a resentful coworker, conflict with superiors in the workplace over ethical issues. Each of these can communicate, by way of their own life stories, what the *Catechism of the Catholic Church* calls "a catechesis of sin and forgiveness" and "a catechesis of grace."[5]

It seems to me, too, that their life stories bear resemblance to the six themes that emerge from the reflections by Fathers O'Keefe, Himes, Vacek, and Billy: the themes of hunger, imagination, gratitude, passion, prodigality, and solidarity. They point as well to a seventh theme, divinization, or "theosis," with which I will conclude. It seems to me that each of these themes will be present in the life of any believer who lives the kind of transfigured life that serves as a sign of the "truth and life," "holiness and grace," "justice, love, and peace" of God's kingdom.

## HUNGER

When Mark O'Keefe writes about the preacher's charge to "interpret the lives of the people of God in biblical light," we must note that people will be open to having their lives interpreted only if they bear within them a certain *hunger for meaning*. Such seems to occur only when our comfortable and familiar self-understandings and/or personal projects implode and collapse. When they do, we can find ourselves free to re-examine our very reason for being.

Kenneth Himes has made a persuasive case that sloth afflicts us and accounts for an alarming contemporary lack of desire to know and experience the content of the moral and spiritual life. Sloth accounts for a widespread moral inertia that is resistant to conscience formation, conversion, and spiritual growth. So, too, I suggest, is another correlate capital sin, gluttony. Expatriate Russian philosopher Mikhail Epstein suggests that we live in a culture characterized by, among other things, hypersexuality, hypersociality, and hypermateriality.[6] Overconsumption submerses us in a world in which our senses are surfeited, and we are too glutted (and entertained) to reflect. Only when we are driven—sometimes by personal dire straits—by the gnawing *hunger for "home"* of the prodigal son (Lk 15:16–32) do we overcome our sloth. As our dulled consciences are awakened, we may realize that our hunger for home is indeed a hunger for the good, a desire for Christ's kingdom.

In our various crises of limits and loneliness, we also experience a *hunger for friendship,* the need for an agapic lover such as God and for the mutuality of the *philia* of which Edward Vacek writes. A pressing question for us, a point for examination of conscience, is where and how the persons in the pews and the students in our lecture halls perceive our church and our practice of religion as invitation to friendship—with God and with the community.

Finally, there is the *hunger for holiness* that persists and perhaps can only be addressed when some of the hunger for meaning, for home (which may also mean hope), and for friendship have begun to be met. Marlene, Bev, Tom, Ted, and Cynthia have been emptied, hollowed out by grief and sin at significant points in their lives. They also live today the "moral mysticism" and the ache for still more of God of which Dennis Billy speaks. As he reminds us, courtesy of Merton, an accessible mysticism may be "the only cure for...angst." The point is that our hungers or "yearnings," as Billy calls them, can and should be appropriately "recognized and dealt with constructively" in the parish, in the theology class, in prayer group and ministerial training, in every possible ecclesial setting.

Both Himes and Billy have warned us that our hungers will not be fed, we will not be nourished, and we will not grow if we lower our expectations of either ourselves and our moral possibilities or our parishes and their formative possibilities. Growth requires imaginative work—which implies the creative exercise of our own dreaming and doing, the creative leadership of pastors and teachers, and the creative interpretations and re-visions of theologians and spiritual writers.

## IMAGINATION

When the Christian is stirred by a hunger for meaning, a hunger for home, a hunger for friendship, and/or a hunger for holiness, he or she, like any hungry person, will be overtaken by visions of feasting. We are familiar with the lush, sensuous descriptions of feasting offered us in scripture (Ps 23:5-6; Prv 9:1-5; Is 55:1-2; Sir 24:18-21; Jn 6:1-14, among them). For our present purposes, I mean by the imagined "feast" an overspilling Christian cornucopia of possibility, the vision of a new life, a new way. It seems to me that O'Keefe, Himes, Vacek, and Billy all suggest that the task of preachers, pastors, catechists, ministers, spiritual directors, teachers, and companions in discipleship is to stimulate the Christian imagination. Only when the Marlenes, Bevs, Toms, Teds, and Cynthias of our world and our church can envision a freeing and finer "What's next?"—only when they can see themselves living a life of discipleship and proceeding step by step along the path to beatitude—only then can they surrender to grace. And only then can they really free themselves from whatever has oppressed or even enslaved them and resist recidivism.

O'Keefe has reminded us of Walter Brueggemann's appeal to preachers to present "a poetic construal of an alternative world." It seems incumbent on all of us, insofar as we all preach by our way of being, that the witness of our lives presents such "a poetic construal" of the kingdom proclaimed by Christ. We need, as Himes suggests, the imaginative stimuli of well wrought hagiography, "standards of heroism," examples of compassion, a rich storytelling of "the lives of ordinary folks who display a quiet heroism." We need the Ignatian art of composition of place and insertion of ourselves into gospel moments. We need meditative experience and meditative memory. We need contemplation.

Philip Keane, a moral theologian not represented in this book, has offered us an exposition of the multiplex meanings of "moral imagination." The emphasis may be on "reconnecting us with our past by the creative use of stories, symbols, traditions, etc.," which is critical in a time of "moral breakdown." Then again, the emphasis may be on "the discovery of new and different ideas," on "dreaming and hoping" for the future, on daring to craft creative solutions to new problems.[7] As Keane suggests, a moral theology based merely on "moral logic or moral principles" may be quite ineffective unless it draws upon the "resources" of "stories, metaphors, vision, playfulness, prayerful reflection, and a virtuous lifestyle."[8] These help to set before seekers a feast. They can also, if we can re-imagine parish along the lines that Billy suggests, help welcome hungry seekers home.

## GRATITUDE

The spiritual writer Brother David Steindl-Rast has written of the relationship between gratitude and surprise. He tells of a moment when he was a child in Austria when bombs began falling as soon as air raid sirens sounded. He rushed into a church, scooted under a pew, and stayed until the Nazi aircraft had left. Once outside, he met smoke and debris. As Brother David tells it,

> that there was anything at all struck me as an overwhelming surprise. My eyes fell on a few square feet of lawn in the midst of all this destruction. It was as if a friend had offered me an emerald in the hollow of his hand. Never before or after have I seen grass so surprisingly green.
>
> Surprise is no more than a beginning of that fullness we call gratefulness.[9]

Brother David calls gratefulness "the heart of prayer" and a "full aliveness to a gratuitously given world."[10] Mark O'Keefe has called "grateful response to God's offer of relationship in Christ" the heart of the moral life. Yet we know from Edward Vacek's treatment of gratitude that he finds it *not* to be the heart of Christian life—love is—but integrally related to our receptivity, relatedness, and generosity, though in admittedly complex ways.

To illustrate gratitude, let me give another example from the lives of ordinary Catholics. This time I will mention Celie, a woman who can be counted on to mutter "Praise you, Jesus; thank you, Jesus," and sometimes to whisper in tongues, every time I lead prayer among the group I meet with on Thursday nights for class. She is praising and thanking God even as we pray for accident victims, the hospitalized, the grieving, the beleaguered president and his family. She is African American, separated from her husband, helping the Salvation Army feed and shelter people, working with youth, using her money for a variety of worthy causes. From what I know of her, I would say that she has seen much of life's smoldering debris. For her, however, its smoke rises like incense. What we perhaps need to recall, amid our theological subtleties, our hermeneutical exercises, and our pastoral complexities is that the human spirit can and does rise amid paschal mystery.

Steindl-Rast has written of the boisterous stillness that is effected when a boys' choir overlays the "interplay between the two halves of a double choir answering one another" in the opening of Bach's "St. Matthew's Passion."[11] Cacophony becomes polyphony, becomes *cantus firmus,* becomes a sounding silence. This image typifies, perhaps, what we most hope for in the moral-spiritual journey, which is sometimes, admittedly, descent into maelstrom or ducking under a blitz. The question is not so much how we teach but how we share our grateful sighs. These mingle with the alleluias and the maranathas of the coming kingdom.

## PASSION

Sidney Callahan, in her study *In Good Conscience,* has attempted what she calls an "expanded definition of conscience," which she considers "holistic." For her, "conscience is a personal, self-conscious activity, integrating reason, emotion, and will in self-committed decisions about right and wrong, good and evil."[12] For her, it is critical that conscience not be defined merely as a kind of "practical reason." Intuition and affect are vital, she believes, because they provide the vision and the passion that impel us, in the end, to act. Our decisions to do things, she reminds us, are enacted "because we emotionally care about them and are personally invested."[13] To put it another way, the doing of good requires passionate caring.

G. Simon Harak elaborates on the same point in his study *Virtuous Passions.* Our richly incarnational tradition, Harak explains, leads us inevitably to the conclusion that morality has a strong affective component. Virtue is activated by our "being moved," specifically by being "moved in the right way, at the right time, to the right extent."[14] Thus, we can properly speak of a "passion for God" and a "passion for justice," Harak observes.[15]

Himes and Billy have spoken quite specifically of the role of passion in the moral life. Being slothful in the sense of being morally apathetic, Himes observes, is to be uncaring and "without passion." Spirituality, for Himes, is a way of reviving our ability to be moved, reawakening passion. "It is by having God move within us that we experience a rebirth of desire and care," he says. Billy imagines the parish as a community in which hearts can burn, as they did in the disciples on the road to Emmaus. His exposition of Fredrica Halligan's *conjunctio* implies not only bonding in community but also a passionate allurement, a drawing together that would seem to require a mutuality of "being moved." The good life, the beatitude evident in the lives of good people like the sojourners I have named in this chapter, can be sustained only if their fire is tended and fed, only if their attachment to God and the company of the kingdom is a passion that is kindled and rekindled again and again.

## PRODIGALITY

It is a kind of gospel truism and an obvious corollary to the two great commandments that love's tendency is to outflow in ever-widening circles. Generosity, as Vacek treats it, in its agapic, erotic, and philiac forms, is, at its fullest, prodigality. Christian loving and Christian giving, he says, tend "to be excessive," to stretch, to extend even "beyond [our] means."

What I would like to suggest here is that prodigality, profligate giving, becomes common practice at a certain point of moral-spiritual development. We respond in love when we have received certain gifts from God: when our hungers have been even moderately fed; when we can imagine a still better, more festive, more spiritually satisfying tomorrow; when we have been overwhelmed with gratitude for the simplest of gifts and come to embrace life itself, our own lives, and other persons; and when we have a zest and energy about the inter-penetration of the divine and the human. The only appropri-ate response to God in light of these experiences is self-giving.

Vacek seems quite right when he suggests that the three types of gifts that we can most meaningfully give God are: ourselves, given in true love; our loving reserve of cer-tain creatures as sacred, sacramental (which implies our protection of them from sacrilegious or trivial use); and, finally, our generous engagement with and giving to others. He nudges us out of spiritual amnesia (to which we all seem bothersomely subject) when he reminds us that God loves "our friends through us"—that our special love of special persons is an embodiment of God's loving. Billy, of course, affirms this in his thoughtful treatment of friendship.

That we can be prodigal lovers, giving beyond our means, can only be true if we are possessed by a certain god-liness. It is, after all, God's own prodigality that is irre-sistible. O'Keefe notes that "God's loving self-offer is always greater than the human potential for refusal," and, of course, we have heard this before. "God is greater than our hearts," notes scripture, and "we love because he first loved us" (1 Jn 3:20, 4:19). We recall, too, John's caution: that our love is false if it excludes, if it bears hatred. We can claim to love God and be found to be liars on the basis of defect in our human loving (1 Jn 4:20).

Himes follows John's logic: We need informed and well-formed consciences in order to make sound moral judgments. If we are not careful in our distinguishing good from bad, right from wrong, and if we settle for mediocrity, we will not become "people who love well." While loving well may require measures of solitude and reflection, we never learn love solo, on our own. We cannot count on a magical infusion of *caritas* to cover over what we have not practiced. For all of us, obviously, loving, giving, and prodigality require community.

## SOLIDARITY

In the preceding essays, some voices have been conspicuously absent—the voices of womanist, feminist, and *mujerista* thinkers about God and the good. If they were here, we might have heard more about the survival and enrichment of the community,[16] risk,[17] "apocalyptic visions of hope and salvation,"[18] *passiones*,[19] autobiography, and ethnography.[20]

Having acknowledged—regretfully so—that there are voices that have not uttered a sound in this book, we still have to affirm that our reflections on morality and spirituality have been all about communion and community. O'Keefe, Himes, Vacek, and Billy have all spoken in one way or another about solidarity—prayer and attentiveness (O'Keefe); intimacy with God, covenantal relatedness, dialogue (Himes); friendship (Vacek and Billy); and deep connectedness with humanity and the earth, as well as with God (Billy). To speak of all of these is to speak of church.

When I reflect on the experiences of Marlene, Bev, Tom, Ted, Cynthia, and Celie, I am convinced that Dennis Billy has struck something vitally important for our future as church. We will be a community where lives are mended and people are strengthened to give only if we are a community among whom people can touch the face of God as they encounter warm, welcoming, flesh-and-blood companions, soul brothers and soul sisters. Reclaiming the root sense of parish as *paroikia,* as the center for exiles and sojourners, will help "build up the kingdom here in our midst...so that peace and justice will one day reign in our little corner of the earth," as Billy suggests. A center for holiness must also be a center of friendships and closely bonded subgroups, a site where faith can be shared, genuine mysticism evoked and enhanced, and where people can be personally known.

The image of church as displaced persons with a definite destination, an *ecclesia* that moves God-ward even as it revels in God-with-us, holds great promise. If people experience church as *paroikia,* in the way that Billy describes it, they would seem amply prepared to face life's ambiguities and blows with assurance. They would also seem equipped to respond with their own moral force to what the United States Bishops' Task Group Summary Report on Catholic social teaching described as that "integral linkage between social justice and spirituality [which] points to a community's whole life in Christ."[21] Where disciples can bond together in prayer, faith, outreach, and intimate self-giving, they build what Stanley Hauerwas has called "a community of character," a school for virtue formed in the Christian story, a locus from which we can widen our worlds,[22] immanently and transcendentally.

## CONCLUSION

As I hope is apparent by now, hunger, imagination, gratitude, passion, prodigality, and solidarity are criteria for a life lived in response to the call to holiness of which Vatican II speaks. They are also hallmarks of the kingdom of God. I am sure that we have exemplars of hungry, imaginative, grateful, passionate, prodigal, and solidaristic disciples among the often inconspicuous yet truly remarkable "moral mystics" in our midst.

This collection of essays represents reflection upon one of our deepest desires—to participate in the life of God and to affirm our urge for ever more of it. In this way, these essays speak of hope, hope that disciples of the Lord who have responded to his call, bonded in the community we call church, and tasted passion, death, and resurrection continue to be a saving leaven in an often cynical and pervasively skeptical culture. In *Tomorrow's Catholic,* Michael Morwood has raised a familiar challenge:

> How do we talk about God in a society that has lost its sense of the sacred, and considers the religious world-view in which we have shaped our images and language about God to be nonsense? How do we talk about Jesus in a society that sees no need for a God-figure to come down from heaven to save us—especially when the salvation is connected with a God who supposedly locked us out of heaven?[23]

Morwood's answer, not surprisingly, is that we must reconstruct our images, reformulate our God-talk, reconceive our Christology. The answer of this book seems, instead, to call us to spend more energy reconstructing, reformulating, and reconceiving our lives.

The Marlenes, Bevs, Toms, Teds, Cynthias, and Celies of our church exemplify in their lives what Mark O'Keefe has developed in *Becoming Good, Becoming Holy,* the themes of *theosis* or *theopoiesis.* This theosis, or divinization, O'Keefe observes, "involves a purifying of the image of God with the goal of realizing the likeness to God."[24] What this means for the seeker, the person of prayer, the believer, is "Christification"—a conforming of one's life to Christ[25] by a life lived in the Spirit, which is also to say a life lived profoundly, intimately, in the church.

"Christification" is, of course, a work already undertaken, the dynamism of the life of every saint, including every saint-in-progress. Moral theologians, pastors, and the faithful at large all have their proper role in the work of the kingdom, the work of "Christification." There are ways that all of us can stimulate, suggest, and model the hunger, imagination, gratitude, passion, prodigality, and solidarity with which we have been concerned here. As Pope John Paul II has reminded us, "the proclamation and presentation of morality" is integral to the "new evangelization." So too is reflection again and again on "the life of holiness which is resplendent in so many members of the People of God, humble and often unseen."[26]

## NOTES

1. Catholic Church, Second Vatican Council, *Lumen Gentium* (Dogmatic Constitution on the Church) #5, in *Vatican Council II: The Conciliar and Post Conciliar Documents*, ed. Austin Flannery, O.P., rev. ed. (Northport, N.Y.: Costello Publishing Company, 1992). (Hereafter *LG*)

2. *LG*, 36.

3. *LG*, 40.

4. Catholic Church, Canadian Bishops, *Statement on the Formation of Conscience* (Boston: Daughters of St. Paul, 1974), 18–23.

5. Catholic Church, *Catechism of the Catholic Church*, trans. from the Latin text from Vatican City: Libreria Editrice Vaticana (Washington, D.C.: United States Catholic Conference, 1994), #1697.

6. Mikhail Epstein, "Hyper in 20th Century Culture: The Dialectics of Transition from Modernism to Postmodernism," *Left Curve* 21 (1997): 5–16.

7. Philip S. Keane, S.S., *Christian Ethics and Imagination: A Theological Inquiry* (Mahwah, N.J.: Paulist Press, 1984), 95–96.

8. Keane, 171.

9. Brother David Steindl-Rast, *Gratefulness, the Heart of Prayer: An Approach to Life in Its Fullness* (Mahwah, N.J.: Paulist Press, 1984), 10.

10. Steindl-Rast, 25.

11. Steindl-Rast, 149.

12. Sidney Callahan, *In Good Conscience: Reason and Emotion in Moral Decision Making* (San Francisco: HarperCollins, 1991), 14.

13. Callahan, 101.

14. G. Simon Harak, S.J., *Virtuous Passions: The Formation of Christian Character* (Mahwah, N.J.: Paulist Press, 1993), 3, 96.

15. Harak, cf. chaps. 5 and 6.

16. Katie G. Cannon, *Black Womanist Ethics* (Atlanta: Scholars Press, 1988).

17. Sharon D. Welch, *A Feminist Ethic of Risk* (Minneapolis: Fortress Press, 1990).

18. Emilie M. Townes, *In a Blaze of Glory: Womanist Spirituality as Social Witness* (Nashville: Abingdon Press, 1995), esp. 139ff.

19. Zaida Maldonado Pérez, "Death and the 'Hour of Triumph': Subversion within the Visions of Saturnus and Polycarp," in *Theology: Expanding the Borders*, eds. Maria Pílar Aquino and Roberto S. Goizueta (Mystic, Conn.: Twenty-Third Publications and the College Theology Society, 1998), 121–44.

20. Marian Ronan, "Reclaiming Women's Experience: A Reading of Selected Christian Feminist Theologies," *Cross Currents* 48 (1998): 218–29.

21. The Task Group Summary Report for the National Conference of Catholic Bishops, *Sharing Catholic Social Teaching: Challenges and Directions–Reflections of the U.S. Catholic Bishops* (Washington, D.C.: United States Catholic Conference, 1998), 13.

22. Cf. Stanley Hauerwas, *A Community of Character: Toward a Constructive Christian Social Ethic* (Notre Dame, Ind.: University of Notre Dame Press, 1981).

23. Michael Morwood, M.S.C., *Tomorrow's Catholic: Understanding God and Jesus in a New Millennium* (Mystic, Conn.: Twenty-Third Publications, 1997), 129.

24. Mark O'Keefe, O.S.B., *Becoming Good, Becoming Holy: On the Relationship of Christian Ethics and Spirituality* (Mahwah, N.J.: Paulist Press, 1995), 60–61.

25. This is an emphasis that appears in John Paul II, *Veritatis Splendor* (The Splendor of Truth) (Boston: Pauline Books and Media, 1993), #21. (Hereafter *VS*)

26. *VS*, 107.

# A Note on the Contributors

*Dennis J. Billy, C.Ss.R., S.T.D.,* is Extraordinary Professor of Moral Theology at the Alphonsian Academy in Rome, Italy. He is the editor of *Spirituality and Morality: Integrating Prayer and Action* with Donna L. Orsuto (Paulist Press, 1996) and the author of *Under the Starry Night: A Wayfarer's Guide Through an Uncertain World* (Ave Maria, 1997).

*Kenneth R. Himes, O.F.M., Ph.D.,* is Professor of Moral Theology at Washington Theological Union and co-editor of *New Theology Review.* He is President-elect of the Catholic Theological Society of America and a theological consultant to the Office of Social Development and World Peace at the United States Catholic Conference. Among his publications are *Fullness of Faith* (Paulist Press, 1993) and *Responses to 101 Questions About Catholic Social Teaching* (Paulist Press, forthcoming).

*James Keating, Ph.D.,* is Associate Professor of Moral Theology in the School of Theology at the Pontifical College Josephinum in Columbus, Ohio. His essays on moral theology and spirituality have appeared in *Pro Ecclesia, Irish Theological Quarterly, Milltown Studies, Religious Studies and*

*Theology*, and *Studies in Spirituality*. He is the author of *Pure Heart, Clear Conscience: Living a Catholic Moral Life* (Our Sunday Visitor, 1999) and co-author with Anthony J. Ciorra of *With Your Whole Heart Turn to God: Moral Formation in the Parish* (Alba House, 1998). Dr. Keating also serves as editor of the *Josephinum Journal of Theology*.

*Mark O'Keefe, O.S.B., S.T.D.*, is President/Rector of St. Meinrad School of Theology in St. Meinrad, Indiana, where he has also served as Associate Professor of Moral Theology since 1987. He is the author of *Becoming Good, Becoming Holy: On the Relationship of Christian Ethics and Spirituality* (Paulist Press, 1995).

*Pamela A. Smith, SS.C.M., Ph.D.*, is Associate Dean, Director of Lay Ministry Programs, and Associate Professor of Systematic and Moral Theology at SS. Cyril and Methodius Seminary in Orchard Lake, Michigan. Her publications include *What Are They Saying About Environmental Ethics?* (Paulist Press, 1997).

*Edward C. Vacek, S.J., Ph.D.*, is Professor of Moral Theology at Weston Jesuit School of Theology in Weston, Massachusetts. He is the author of *Love, Human and Divine: The Heart of Christian Ethics* (Georgetown University Press, 1994).

# Select Bibliography

## BOOKS

Anderson, E. Byron, and Bruce T. Morrill, eds. *Liturgy and the Moral Self.* Collegeville, Minn.: Liturgical Press, 1998.

Ashley, Benedict, O.P. *Living the Truth in Love: A Biblical Introduction to Moral Theology.* New York: Alba House, 1996.

Billy, Dennis J. *Under the Starry Night: A Wayfarer's Guide Through an Uncertain World.* Notre Dame, Ind.: Ave Maria Press, 1997.

Billy, Dennis J., and Donna L. Orsuto, eds. *Spirituality and Morality: Integrating Prayer and Action.* Mahwah, N.J.: Paulist Press, 1996.

Bretzke, James T., S.J. *Bibliography on Scripture and Christian Ethics.* Studies in Religion and Society Ser. 39. Lewiston, N.Y.: The Edwin Mellen Press, 1997.

Brown, Neil. *Spirit of the World: The Moral Basis of Christian Spirituality.* Manly, New South Wales, Australia: Catholic Institute of Sydney, 1990.

Burgard, Stephen. *Hallowed Ground: Rediscovering Our Spiritual Roots.* New York: Insight Books, 1997.

Catholic Church, National Conference of Catholic Bishops. *Principal as Spiritual Leader: Expectations in the Areas of Faith Development, Building Christian Community, Moral and Ethical Development, History and Philosophy.* Maria J. Ciriello, ed. Washington, D.C.: Department of Education, United States Catholic Conference, 1996.

Ciorra, Anthony J., and James Keating, *With Your Whole Heart Turn to God: Moral Formation in the Parish.* New York: Alba House, 1998.

Cover, Jeanne. *Love–The Driving Force: Mary Ward's Spirituality: It's Significance for Moral Theology.* Marquette, Wisc.: Marquette University Press [1997].

Duffey, Michael K. *Be Blessed in What You Do: The Unity of Christian Ethics and Spirituality.* Mahwah, N.J.: Paulist Press, 1988.

Gula, Richard. *The Good Life: Where Morality and Spirituality Converge.* Mahwah, N.J.: Paulist Press, 1999.

———. *Moral Discernment.* Mahwah, N.J.: Paulist Press, 1997.

———. *Reason Informed by Faith.* Mahwah, N.J.: Paulist Press, 1989.

Guroian, Vigen. *Ethics After Christendom: Toward an Ecclesial Christian Ethic.* Grand Rapids, Mich.: Eerdmans, 1994.

Hanson, Bradley, ed. *Modern Christian Spirituality: Methodological and Historical Essays.* American Academy of Religion: Studies in Religion Ser. 62. Atlanta: Scholars Press, 1990.

Hayes, Richard. *The Moral Vision of the New Testament.* San Francisco: Harper, 1996.

Heschel, Abraham Joshua. *Moral Grandeur and Spiritual Audacity: Essays.* New York: Farrar, Straus, & Giroux, 1996.

Himes, Kenneth, O.F.M., and Michael J Himes. *Fullness of Faith: The Public Significance of Theology.* Mahwah, N.J.: Paulist Press, 1993.

Horne, James R. *The Moral Mystic.* Waterloo, Ontario, Canada: Wilfrid Laurier University Press, 1983.

Horton, John, and Susan Mendus. *After MacIntyre: Critical Perspectives on the Work of Alasdair MacIntyre.* Notre Dame, Ind.: University of Notre Dame Press, 1994.

Keating, James. *Pure Heart–Clear Conscience: Living a Catholic Moral Life.* Huntington, Ind.: Our Sunday Visitor, 1999.

Kennedy, Terence, C.Ss.R. *Doers of the Word: Moral Theology for the Third Millennium.* Liguori, Mo.: Triumph Books, 1995.

Kinsley, David R. *Ecology and Religion: Ecological Spirituality in Cross-Cultural Perspective.* Englewood Cliffs, N.J.: Prentice Hall, 1995.

O'Keefe, Mark, O.S.B. *Becoming Good, Becoming Holy: On the Relationship of Christian Ethics and Spirituality.* Mahwah, N.J.: Paulist Press, 1995.

Paris, Peter J. *The Spirituality of African Peoples: The Search for a Common Moral Discourse.* Minneapolis: Fortress Press, 1995.

Patrick, Anne E. *Liberating Conscience: Feminist Explorations in Catholic Moral Theory.* New York: Continuum, 1996.

Peck, M. Scott. *Denial of the Soul: Spiritual and Medical Perspectives on Euthanasia and Mortality.* New York: Harmony Books, 1997.

Purpel, David E. *The Moral and Spiritual Crisis in Education: A Curriculum for Justice and Compassion in Education.* New York: Bergin and Garvey, 1989.

Smith, Harmon L. *Where Two or Three Are Gathered: Liturgy and the Moral Life.* Cleveland: Pilgrim Press, 1995.

Spohn, William. *What Are They Saying about Scripture and Ethics?* Mahwah, N.J.: Paulist Press, 1995.

————. *Go and Do Likewise: Jesus and Ethics.* New York: Continuum, 1999.

Stock, Brian. *Augustine the Reader: Meditation, Self-Knowledge, and the Ethics of Interpretation.* Cambridge, Mass.: Harvard University Press, 1996.

Vacek, Edward C. *Love, Human and Divine: The Heart of Christian Ethics.* Washington, D.C.: Georgetown University Press, 1994.

Vidal, Marciano. *Moral y espiritualidad: de la separación a la convergencia.* Madrid: Editorial El Perpetuo Socorro, 1997.

Wadell, Paul J. *The Primacy of Love.* Mahwah, N.J: Paulist Press, 1992.

————. *Friends of God: Virtues and Gifts in Aquinas.* New York: P. Lang, 1991.

————. *Friendship and the Moral Life.* Notre Dame, Ind.: University of Notre Dame Press, 1989.

## ARTICLES

Bexell, Göran. "Theological Interpretation of Biblical Texts on Moral Issues." *Studia Theologica: Scandinavian Journal of Theology* 51 (1997): 3–14.

Billy, Dennis J., C.Ss.R. "The Person of the Holy Spirit as the Source of the Christian Moral Life." *Studia Moralia* 36 (December 1998): 325–59.

————. "A 'Spiritual Turn' for Catholic Moral Theology," *Review for Religious* 57 (November-December 1998): 595–604.

————. "Mysticism and Moral Theology." *Studia Moralia* 34 (December 1996): 389–415.

Carr, Elizabeth E. M. "The Fire Within: Discovering Adult Freedom Before God." *The Way Supplement* 88 (Spring 1997): 107–16.

Cunningham, Lawrence S. "Practicing Ethics and Spirituality." *Commonweal* 116 (October 20, 1989): 572–74.

Duffey, Michael K. "Called to be Holy: The Reconvergence of Christian Morality and Spirituality." *Spirituality Today* 38 (Winter 1986): 349–60.

Endean, Philip. "Moral Theology, Karl Rahner and the Ignatian Exercises." *The Way Supplement* 88 (Spring 1997): 55–65.

Ginter, Mark E. "The Holy Spirit and Morality." *Proceedings of the Catholic Theological Society of America* 51 (1996): 165–79.

————. "Conscience and the Holy Spirit." *Logos: A Journal of Eastern Christian Studies* 36 (1995): 7–30.

Griffiths, Leslie. "Sermons and Ethics." *The Way Supplement* 88 (Spring 1997): 77–85.

Gustafson, James M. "The Use of Scripture in Christian Ethics." *Studia Theologica: Scandinavian Journal of Theology* 51 (1997): 15–29.

Hanigan, James P. "Conscience and the Holy Spirit." *Proceedings of the Catholic Theological Society of America* 51 (1996): 227–46.

————. "Militant Nonviolence: A Spirituality for the Pursuit of Social Justice." *Horizons* 9 (Spring 1982): 7–22.

————. "Conscience: An Ethical and Spiritual Reality." *Listening* 34, no. 3 (Fall, 1999).

Hepburn, Liz. "Bioethics and the Spiritual." *The Way Supplement* 88 (Spring 1997): 86–94.

Himes, Kenneth, O.F.M. "Justice-and-Peace Ministry: Three Decades Plus." *Review for Religious* 56 (May-June 1997): 251–67.

————. "The Inextricable Link of Charity and Discipleship." *Origins* 26 (February 20, 1996): 573–78.

————. "The Contribution of Theology to Catholic Moral Theology," 48–73 in Charles Curran, ed. *Moral Theology: Challenges for the Future.* Mahwah, N.J.: Paulist Press, 1990.

————. "The Relationship of Religion and Morality." *Social Thought* 15 (Summer-Fall 1989): 33–41.

————. "Eucharist and Justice: Assessing the Legacy of Virgil Michel." *Worship* 62 (May 1988): 201–24.

————. "Prayer and the Moral Life: Tracing the Connection." *Listening* 34, no. 3 (Fall, 1999).

Hogan, Linda. "Gender and Ethics in Spirituality." *The Way Supplement* 88 (Spring 1997): 95–106.

Johnston, Carol. "Essential Connections: Spirituality and Justice in a Reformed Perspective." *Church and Society* 83 (November-December 1992): 33–41.

Jones, H. Kimball. "Confronting the Shadow: A Jungian Perspective on Spirituality and Ethics." *Journal of Humanism and Ethical Religion* 4 (Fall 1991): 41–62.

Keane, Philip. "The Role of the Holy Spirit in Contemporary Moral Theology." *Proceedings of the Catholic Theological Society of America* 51 (1996): 97–113.

Keating, James. "Evangelizing Conscience: Taking on the Mind of Christ." *Pro Ecclesia* 8 (Fall 1999): 475–87.

————. "The Conscience Imperative as Prayer." *Irish Theological Quarterly* 63 (1998): 65–89.

————. "Open to the Divine: Prayer and Morality in the Thought of Enda McDonagh." *Religious Studies and Theology* 16:2 (December 1997): 19–36.

————. "Listening to Christ's Heart: Moral Theology and Spirituality in Dialogue." *Milltown Studies* 39 (Summer 1997): 48–65.

————. "Karl Rahner: Prayer and Ethics." *Studies in Spirituality* 7 (July 1997): 163–77.

————. "Prayer and Ethics in the Thought of Hans Urs Von Balthasar." *Irish Theological Quarterly* 62 (1996/97): 29–37.

————. "The Good Life: An Invitation to Holiness." *Church* 11 (Summer 1995): 15–20.

Keenan, James F. "The Meaning of Suffering," in Alan Faden and Edmund Pellegrino, eds., *Jewish Medical Ethics.* Washington, D.C.: Georgetown University Press, forthcoming.

————. "Morality and Spirituality: What's The Difference?" in Todd Salzmann, ed., *Method and Catholic Moral Theology: The Ongoing Reconstruction.* Omaha: Creighton University Press, 1999.

————. "Catholic Moral Theology, Ignatian Spirituality, and Virtue Ethics: Strange Bedfellows." *The Way Supplement* 88 (Spring 1997): 36–45.

————. "Rooting Morality in Spirituality." *Church* 12:4 (1996): 38–40.

————. "Listening to the Voice of Suffering." *Church* 12:3 (1996): 41–43.

————. "Prayer and the Moral Life." *Church* 12:2 (1996): 38–40.

————. "Ethics and Spirituality: Historical Distinctions and Contemporary Challenges." *Listening* 34, no. 3 (Fall, 1999).

Lamb, Matthew L. "Christian Spirituality and Social Justice." *Horizons* 10 (Spring 1983): 32–49.

Langston, Douglas. "The Spark of Conscience: Bonaventure's View of Conscience and Synderesis." *Franciscan Studies* 53 (1993; c. 1997): 79–95.

Lee, Dorothy A. "Scripture, Ethics and Spirituality." *The Way Supplement* 88 (Spring 1997): 16–25.

MacNamara, Vincent. "The Moral Journey." *The Way Supplement* 88 (Spring 1997): 6–15.

O'Day, Gail R. "The Ethical Shape of Pauline Spirituality." *Brethren Life and Thought* 32 (Spring 1987): 81–92.

O'Keefe, Mark, O.S.B. "Merton's 'True Self' and the Fundamental Option," pp. 235–50 in Victor A. Kramer, ed. *The Merton Annual.* Vol. 10 (1997). Collegeville, Minn.: Liturgical Press, 1998.

————. "The Unity of Christian Morality and Spirituality: A Benedictine Witness." *The American Benedictine Review* 48 (March 1997): 3–18.

————. "The Holy Spirit in the Monastic Tradition." *Proceedings of the Catholic Theological Society of America* 51 (1996): 199–204.

————. "Ministry for a Good and Holy People." *The Priest* 51 (June 1995): 12–15.

————. "Christian Prayer and Moral Decision-Making." *Spiritual Life* 40 (Autumn 1994): 169–78.

————. "Catholic Moral Theology and Christian Spirituality." *New Theology Review* 7 (May 1994): 60–73.

————. "Theosis and the Christian Life: Toward Integrating Roman Catholic Ethics and Spirituality." *Eglise et Théologie* 25:1 (1994): 47–63.

————. "The Ideal of Holiness and the Shape of the Christian Moral Life." *Listening* 34, no. 3 (Fall, 1999).

Overberg, Kenneth. "Christian Ethics and the Spiritual Director." *Presence: The Journal of Spiritual Directors International* 3:2 (May 1997): 47–56.

Patrick, Anne E. "Ethics and Spirituality: The Social Justice Connection." *The Way Supplement* 63 (Fall 1988): 103–16.

Pawlikowski, John T. "Spirituality and the Quest for Justice," in Daniel F. Polish and Eugene J. Fisher, eds., *Liturgical Foundations of Social Policy in the Catholic and Jewish Traditions* (Notre Dame, Ind.: University of Notre Dame Press, 1983) 79–97.

Pinckaers, O.P., Servais. "'In the Beginning Was the Word': Scripture and the Renewal of Moral Theology." *Catholic International* 8:5 (May 1997): 217–23.

Porter, Jean. "Virtue Ethics and Its Significance for Spirituality." *The Way Supplement* 88 (Spring 1997): 26–35.

Ruffing, Janet K. "Unacknowledged Conflicts: Prayer and Morality." *The Way Supplement* 88 (Spring 1997): 66–76.

Schneiders, Sandra M. "Theology and Spirituality: Strangers, Rivals, or Partners?" *Horizons* 13:2 (Fall 1986): 253–74.

Smith, Pamela, SS.C.M. "Conversion à la James: Some Contemporary Applications." *American Benedictine Review* 45 (1994): 62–73.

Spohn, William. "Spirituality and Ethics: Exploring the Connections." *Theological Studies* 58 (1997): 109–23.

————. "Beatitudes and Woes." *Journal of Spiritual Formation* 15 (1994): 35–45.

Vacek, Edward C. "Religious Life and the Eclipse of Love for God." *Review for Religious* 57:2 (March-April 1998): 118–37.

————. "Divine Command, Natural-Law, and Mutual-Love Ethics." *Theological Studies* 57:4 (December 1996): 633–53.

————. "Love for God—Is it Obligatory?" *The Annual of the Society of Christian Ethics,* ed. Society of Christian Ethics and Harlan Beckley (Chicago: Society of Christian Ethics, c. 1996): 221–47.

————. "The Eclipse of Love for God." *America* 174:8 (March 9, 1996): 13–16.

————. "Never on Sunday: Whatever Happened to Leisure." *Commonweal* 121:3 (February 11, 1994): 13–16.

————. "John Paul II and Cooperation with God." *The Annual of the Society of Christian Ethics,* ed. Society of Christian Ethics, and D.M. Yeager, et al. (Knoxville, Tenn.: Society of Christian Ethics, Dept. of Religious Studies, University of Tennessee, 1990): 81–108.

————. "Toward a Phenomenology of Love Lost." *Journal of Phenomenological Psychology* 20:1 (Spring 1989): 1–19.

————. "Personal Growth and the '*Ordo Amoris*'." *Listening* 21:3 (Fall 1986): 197–209.

————. "God's Action and Ours." *Emmanuel* 90:7 (September 1984): 370–76.

————. "Popular Ethical Subjectivism: Four Preludes to Objectivity." *Horizons* 11:1 (Spring 1984): 42–60.

Wadell, Paul. "The Practice of Friendship in the Christian Moral and Spiritual Life: Retrieving the Vision of Aquinas." *Listening* 34, no. 3 (Fall, 1999).